Spenser and Literary Pictorialism

NON SINE SOLE
IRIS

The "Rainbow" Portrait of Queen Elizabeth I
Artist Unknown, c.1600
Marquess of Salisbury, Hatfield House

Published by courtesy of the Marquess of Salisbury, K.G.

BY JOHN B. BENDER

Spenser and Literary Pictorialism

PRINCETON UNIVERSITY PRESS

Copyright © 1972 by Princeton University Press
Library of Congress Card: 71-166361
International Standard Book Number: 0-691-06211-0

Publication of this book has been aided by the Whitney Darrow
Publication Reserve Fund of Princeton University Press

This book has been composed in Linotype Granjon
Printed in the United States of America
by Princeton University Press, Princeton, New Jersey

To the Memory of My Father

Preface

The title of this book perhaps implies that the reader should expect to find here a comprehensive treatment of two immense subjects. I must dash any such hopes, or fears, at once. So many general works by talented critics of Spenser have appeared during the last decade that another hardly seems necessary, and the handful of really useful works on literary pictorialism is so small that the student who contemplates a broadly historical, theoretical, and critical treatise on the subject must envision as well a lifetime of preparatory research.

Instead of a double treatise, I offer the reader an essay in which a few propositions about the nature of literary pictorialism are discussed and a few specific varieties of this pervasive phenomenon are illustrated by comparing Spenser's use of visual materials with that of other writers: Chaucer, Shakespeare, Milton, Keats, Flaubert. In particular, Spenser's extensive imitation of Ariosto and Tasso is the occasion for detailed comparison of their descriptive and illustrative imagery with his representation of visual process.

Any comprehensive study of literary pictorialism would have to order one of the most chaotic attics in the house of literary criticism, so I find it intellectually defensible, as well as practical, to have begun with one corner: I propose a new approach and a new terminology, both of which need to be tested by a larger audience than that composed of the friends and teachers, colleagues and students who have read the work, or parts of it, during its composition.

Even this small, private audience is too numerous to be catalogued here, but I should like at least to name those who have been burdened with some version of the entire work. In a special class is Robert Martin Adams, who has commented generously and wisely on every version. My first and greatest debt is to him, for his belief that I might make something of the subject and for his refusal to be easily satisfied. I am also particularly grateful to Paul J. Alpers, who first offered an enormously helpful anonymous commentary and later emerged to give advice *in propria persona*, and to Thomas P. Roche, Jr., who encouraged me at a time when progress on the work was stalled. I am much indebted to other sympathetic though properly skeptical critics including Evalynn Monsky, Wesley Trimpi, Joseph B. Dallett, Ronald Rebholz, Herbert Lindenberger, and J. Martin Evans, whose close readings yielded a wealth of detailed advice; and besides to George F. Sensabaugh, David Halliburton, and Scott Elledge for their helpful readings of the work. I owe thanks as well to Mrs. Martyn Hitchcock of Princeton University Press for her understanding and keen advice while the manuscript was becoming a book.

Ian Watt, as chairman of the English Department at Stanford, received and most generously granted my requests for travel and research funds during the composition. Help with the research came from Tony Harrison and Joan Bennett. I also wish to thank the librarians of the Warburg Institute, the Henry E. Huntington Library, the British Museum, and the Cornell and Stanford University Libraries for their knowledge and patience. The "Rainbow" Portrait of Queen Elizabeth I is reproduced by permission of the Marquess of Salisbury, and the translations of Ariosto are quoted by permission of Allan Gilbert.

Finally, and most especially, it is a pleasure to mention my wife, who has spent many hours in pursuit of those most unpleasant tasks in book-making—proofreading and comforting the disconsolate author.

John B. Bender

Tours

June, 1971

FREQUENTLY CITED EDITIONS
AND TRANSLATIONS

Ludovico Ariosto. *Orlando furioso*, ed. Santorre Debenedetti and Cesare Segre. Bologna: Commissione per i Testi di Lingua, 1960.

Ludovico Ariosto. *Orlando Furioso*, trans. Allan Gilbert, 2 vols. New York, 1954.

Torquato Tasso. *Opere, III, Gerusalemme liberata,* ed. Bruno Maier. Milan: Rizzoli Editore, 1963.

Torquato Tasso. *Jerusalem Delivered*, trans. Edward Fairfax. Carbondale, Ill., 1962.

Edmund Spenser. *The Works of Spenser: A Variorum Edition,* ed. Edwin Greenlaw, Charles G. Osgood, Frederick M. Padelford, *et al.*, 11 vols. Baltimore, 1932-1957. Cited as *Variorum,* followed by volume number and page or line references. Citations of *The Faerie Queene* appear in the text (Book. Canto. Stanza).

CONTENTS

Spenser and Literary Pictorialism

CHAPTER ONE

Introduction

My general purpose is to theorize and illustrate some formal and rhetorical solutions to the problem of embodying visual experience in poetic language. My analysis, although it concentrates upon Spenser, is intended to provide prolegomena to a critical history of pictorial rhetoric which would classify the diverse uses of visual materials in poetry. Such a history might now be written. Recent studies of perception and the visual arts can guide us to definitions of pictorial devices in literature based upon less elusive critical metaphors than those commonplace in the *ut pictura poesis* tradition following Horace or in the aesthetic tradition of sharp neo-classic distinction between temporal and spatial arts established by Lessing. Horace's simile, misunderstood and removed from context, was one of the chief topoi of Renaissance literary theory but it has ordinarily been the occasion for whimsy in practical criticism. Likewise, only by extreme metaphorical extension of terms could poetry be said to imitate the frozen moments of visual experience granted to painting by Lessing. His notion of painting has been corrected, but we still need detailed comparisons between literature and the other arts which, as Giovanni Giovannini says, presume that "extensive differences in the materials used (words, stone, pigments, etc.) impose on each art a complexity peculiar to it and outside the area of affinity."[1] We must recognize what-

---

[1] "Method in the Study of Literature and Its Relation to the Other Arts," *JAAC*, viii (1950), 193; an excellent treatment of the scholarship in the field, but largely negative. Giovannini calls for a comprehensive theory of the analyzable correspondences among the arts. He leaves us with the depressing idea that almost every attempted method has been "insufficiently grounded in what is relevant and analyzable" (p. 191).

ever affinities actually exist instead of insisting upon entirely consistent parallels between the arts.

The particular concern of this study is to discriminate between the descriptive and the pictorial in poetry. I shall discuss several kinds of pictorial vision in the works of Spenser and other authors whose pictorialism depends less upon massive descriptive detail than upon exact and definable rhetorical molding of visual materials. Spenser's many pictorial effects and devices are grouped under three headings: "Focusing"—reiterated visual imagery fixed into sequences analogous to the process of vision; "Framing"—formally or spatially coherent visual fields suspended at points of marked interruption or reversal of action; "Scanning"—rapidly juxtaposed image clusters and spatial fragments which shatter visual experience into sequential units. The consistent or systematic application of definitions is difficult, and only occasionally will Spenser's imagery fall precisely into these patterns, which he usually combines with more diffuse visual materials and more familiar literary devices. His poetry is sometimes pictorial—sometimes iconic, allegorical, logical, or descriptive—and ordinarily it is several such things at once. Poetry seldom if ever depends solely upon pictorialism for its effect, for the poet always remains a verbal artist who cannot surrender rhetorical contact with his audience.

Ut Pictura Poesis and the Nature of Spenser's Imagery

John Dryden's preface to his translation of Charles du Fresnoy's *De Arte Graphica* contains most of the Renaissance commonplaces about the relationship between poetry and painting:

> For the moral (as Bossu observes) is the first business of the poet, as being the ground-work of his instruction. This being formed, he contrives such a design or fable, as may be

most suitable to the moral. After this he begins to think of the persons whom he is to employ in carrying on his design; and gives them the manners which are most proper to their several characters. The thoughts and words are the last parts, which give beauty and colouring to the piece.

Expression, and all that belongs to words, is that in a poem which colouring is in a picture. The colours well chosen in their proper places, together with the lights and shadows which belong to them, lighten the design, and make it pleasing to the eye. The words, the expressions, the tropes and figures, the versification, and all the other elegancies of sound, as cadences, turns of words upon the thought, and many other things which are all parts of expression, perform exactly the same office both in dramatic and epic poetry.[2]

The theoretical correspondences between pictorial design and poetic plot, color and verbal expression, upon which Dryden bases his "Parallel of Poetry and Painting" are unfortunately so imprecise and difficult to apply that his practical criticism becomes almost entirely impressionistic: for example, he compares Titian and Correggio, the leading Venetian colorists, to Virgil, the most subtle epic stylist.[3] Such misleading par-

[2] "A Parallel of Poetry and Painting" in *Of Dramatic Poesy and Other Critical Essays,* ed. George Watson (London and New York, 1962), II, 186 and 203. These commonplaces, and the attack upon them in the eighteenth century, have a complex history which has been traced by excellent historians of literature and art. In this chapter, and elsewhere, I am particularly indebted to Jean H. Hagstrum, *The Sister Arts* (Chicago and London, 1958), and to Rensselaer W. Lee, "*Ut Pictura Poesis*: The Humanistic Theory of Painting," *Art Bulletin,* XXII (1940), 197-269. Mario Praz, *Mnemosyne: The Parallel between Literature and the Visual Arts* (Princeton, 1970), would certainly have been helpful but it appeared too late.

[3] *Critical Essays,* II, 203-204. Lee, p. 202, says that the Italian critics never really fastened on the idea of purely formal correspondences, a notion overworked by the French and English. He says that the statement opening Charles du Fresnoy's poem (Paris, 1667) remains "the

Introduction

allels are probably an inevitable result of any attempt to establish a detailed system of correspondence between painting and poetry. In the Renaissance, at least, the theoretical attempt to establish a close identity between them proceeded at such a high level of abstraction that it provided little guidance for actual comparisons. The arts were thought to differ "in means and manner of expression, but were considered almost identical in fundamental nature, in content, and in purpose."[4] Comparative studies of the two arts inevitably rely upon various analogies, but most comparisons in the Renaissance were ultimately based upon a few adages from antiquity which provided little guidance to the fanciful critical imagination.

Although Aristotle and Horace say little about relationships between the arts, their few observations strongly influenced Renaissance critics. Aristotle distinguishes between them according to the *means* of imitation employed.[5] He is aware that the correspondences he implies are metaphorical, and he clearly intends his comparisons to be no more than illustrations. For example: "We maintain, therefore, that the first essential, the life and soul, so to speak, of Tragedy is the Plot; and that the Characters come second—compare the parallel in painting, where the most beautiful colours laid on without order will not give one the same pleasure as a simple black-and-white sketch of a portrait" (1450a-1450b). He emphasizes not equivalences

---

best single text for the entire doctrine based on *ut pictura poesis*, citing as it does both the Horatian simile and the saying of Simonides [that painting is mute poetry and poetry a speaking picture—attributed to him by Plutarch], and declaring in effect that painting, since unworthy subject matter concerns it no more than it does poetry, has an equal status with poetry as a liberal art" (p. 197, n. 5).

[4] Lee, p. 197.

[5] *Poetics*, trans. Ingram Bywater (New York, 1954), 1447a. On the ancient tradition of comparisons between the arts see Hagstrum, pp. 3-36; my account depends very heavily upon these pages.

between formal elements of tragedy and painting, but order as the most important principle in any work of art.[6] Aristotle distinguished carefully among the arts, but his comparisons later seemed to lend authority to systems of formal correspondences. Horace, too, was less extravagant in his comparison of painting and poetry than we might guess from the Renaissance doctrine based upon his famous words, "ut pictura poesis." The phrase appears in a passage of the *Ars Poetica* the import of which appears to be that poems, like paintings, vary in mood and type, and that our interest in a good poem is similar to our interest in a good picture.

> Ut pictura poesis: erit quae, si propius stes,
> te capiat magis, et quaedam, si longius abstes.
> haec amat obscurum, volet haec sub luce videri,
> iudicis argutum quae non formidat acumen;
> haec placuit semel, haec deciens repetita placebit.

(A poem is like a picture: one strikes your fancy more, the nearer you stand; another, the farther away. This courts the shade, that will wish to be seen in the light, and dreads not the critic insight of the judge. This pleased but once; that, though ten times called for, will always please.)[7]

[6] Hagstrum, pp. 6-7, discusses this point.

[7] *Satires, Epistles and Ars Poetica*, ed. and trans. H. Rushton Fairclough (Cambridge, Mass. and London, 1929), ll.361-365. Horace's lines have never been fully explicated. Perhaps they never will be, for according to C. O. Brink, *Horace on Poetry* (Cambridge, 1963), p. 247, Horace seems purposely to avoid using the technical language of literary criticism in the *Ars Poetica*; here is Brink's synopsis of the lines: "Certain poems, like certain paintings, are so well made that they satisfy repeated inspection and delight more than once" (p. 258). Another critic, however, observing that Horace's context is a discussion of Homer and the long poem, argues that "poesis" is used here as a critical term referring to the extended poem with a unified subject; Horace's remarks, then, would refer to the different styles used

Introduction

This statement is very different from du Fresnoy's bold announcement as translated by Dryden: "Painting and Poesy are two sisters, which are so like in all things, that they mutually lend to each other, both their name and office. One is called a dumb poesy, and the other a speaking picture."[8] Dryden and du Fresnoy are only late examples of the pervasive Renaissance embellishment of illustrative comparisons made by ancient authorities.

In addition to the rather casual comparisons between painting and poetry made by Aristotle and Horace, there was, especially in later antiquity, an influential tradition of parallels between the arts.[9] Central to this tradition was the rhetorical term *enargeia*, which referred to the orator's power to evoke objects and scenes in the minds of his listeners by the use of vivid imagery. Aristotle, as Hagstrum says, uses not this term but the homonymous word *energeia* (*Rhetoric*, 1410b-1412a), and

---

in a single long poem and to the familiar idea that the many lines in an epic cannot be wrought as finely as the few in a short poem or "poema." See Anthos Ardizzoni, ΠΟΙΗΜΑ: *Ricerche sulla teoria del linguaggio poetico nell'antichità* (Bari, 1953), p. 39, *et passim*.

[8] *The Works of John Dryden*, ed. Sir Walter Scott and George Saintsbury (London, 1892), xvii, 342-343:

> Ut pictura poesis erit; similisque poesi
> Sit pictura; refert par aemula quaeque sororem,
> Alternantque vices et nomina; muta poesis
> Dicitur haec, pictura loquens solet illa vocari.

Until the mid-sixteenth century, the crucial line was punctuated, "Ut pictura poesis erit;" etc. On the important influence of the error see Hagstrum, pp. 59-60, 174-175. Research in early editions by my colleague Wesley Trimpi indicates that the majority of Renaissance critics of Horace take all three of his points evaluatively, even though the first at least appears not to imply comparative evaluation; they ordinarily do not analyze part one of the passage as a statement about optics in painting, even though they understand its reference.

[9] According to Hagstrum, pp. 59-61, this late-antique tradition was partly codified by Plutarch and Philostratus, and was carried along into the Renaissance with the late glosses and commentaries on the *Ars Poetica*.

Ut Pictura Poesis *and* Imagery

refers to the "actualization of potency, the realization of capacity or capability, the achievement in art and rhetoric of the dynamic and purposive life of nature," not to "the achievement in verbal discourse of a natural quality or of a pictorial quality that is highly natural [*enargeia*]" (p. 12). Like Aristotle's idea that imitation in art is the achievement of an organic and self-consistent unity parallel to but not identical in medium or detail with what it imitates, his concept of "vividness" depends upon an inner liveliness and consistency, not upon faithfulness to outward forms. Aristotle is more concerned with the final effect that imitations achieve by their own organic coherence, than with exact correspondence of details to the surfaces of reality.[10]

By Horace's time, the concept of imitation came to include a commitment to verisimilitude, that is, to the naturalistic rendering of the visible world. The non-Aristotelian concept of *enargeia* or liveliness was essential to mimesis so conceived. This naturalistic idea of poetic and painterly imitation prevalent in later antiquity dominated the Renaissance, and perhaps explains why certain Renaissance literary critics equate *energeia* and *enargeia*—sometimes even speaking of the latter as a general characteristic of true poetic style.[11] The vivid rep-

[10] S. H. Butcher, *Aristotle's Theory of Poetry and Fine Art . . .* , 4th ed. (New York, 1951), Chapter Two, "Imitation as an Aesthetic Term."

[11] George Chapman, for example: "That, *Enargia*, or cleerenes of representation, requird in absolute Poems is not the perspicuous deliuery of a lowe inuention; but high, and harty inuention exprest in most significant, and vnaffected phrase; it serues not a skilfull Painters turne, to draw the figure of a face onely to make knowne who it represents; but hee must lymn, giue luster, shaddow, and heightening; which though ignorants will esteeme spic'd, and too curious, yet such as haue the iudiciall perspectiue, will see it hath, motion, spirit and life. . . .

"Obscuritie in affection of words, & indigested concets, is pedanticall and childish; but where it shroudeth it selfe in the hart of his subiect, vtterd with fitnes of figure, and expressiue Epethites; with that darknes

9

Introduction

resentation of reality, as Hagstrum says, could be achieved better in painting than in poetry, and poets claiming to imitate an idealized Nature could hardly fail to endorse the critical dogma that poetry should resemble painting (p. 10). The theory of painting had even more to gain, for painting, unlike poetry, was still struggling for the status of a liberal art in the Renaissance. The central purpose of the close association of poetry and painting in humanistic art theory, as Rensselaer Lee observes, was the elevation of painting to the eminence that poetry had enjoyed for centuries. In the absence of a coherent ancient theory of painting, art theorists turned to Aristotle and Horace, and they "did not hesitate to appropriate as the foundation of their own theory many basic concepts of the two ancient treatises, making them apply in a more or less Procrustean manner to the art of painting for which they were never intended."[12]

wil J still labour to be shaddowed." *The Poems of George Chapman*, ed. Phyllis Brooks Bartlett (New York and London, 1941), p. 49. This passage is analyzed from slightly different points of view in discussions of *enargeia* by Rosemond Tuve, *Elizabethan and Metaphysical Imagery* (Chicago, 1947), pp. 29-32; Hagstrum, pp. 62-65; and Paul J. Alpers, *The Poetry of The Faerie Queene* (Princeton, 1967), pp. 102-106. Baxter Hathaway, *The Age of Criticism* (Ithaca, 1962), pp. 9-22 treats *enargeia* in Italian criticism. On the term *enargeia*, or "forcibleness," see Neil L. Rudenstine, *Sidney's Poetic Development* (Cambridge, Mass., 1967), pp. 149-171. Alpers argues that English critics tend to equate or confuse *enargeia* with *energeia*, whereas Italian critics use it more in the traditional rhetorical sense defined by Quintilian when he says that it "makes us seem not so much to narrate as to exhibit the actual scene, while our emotions will be no less actively stirred than if we were present at the actual occurrence." *Institutio Oratoria*, tr. H. E. Butler, 4 vols. (Cambridge, Mass. and London, 1920-1922), Book VI, 2, 32; see also IV, 2, 63-64 and VIII, 3, 61-62. Hagstrum, pp. 9-12, cites Quintilian and other ancient writers on *enargeia* in his discussion of the concept of imitation in later antiquity. When I use the term, it will be in Quintilian's sense.

[12] Lee, pp. 201-202. John R. Spencer, "*Ut Rhetorica Pictura*: a Study in Quattrocento Theory of Painting," *JWCI*, XX (1957), 26-44, has

Ut Pictura Poesis *and Imagery*

Two English writers from Spenser's time can exemplify the routine application of *ut pictura poesis.* In the Argument to "Februarie" in the *Shepheardes Calender,* E. K. says that "the olde man telleth a tale of the Oake and the Bryer, so liuely and so feelingly, as if the thing were set forth in some Picture before our eyes, more plainly could not appeare." This obviously is a reference to the concept of *enargeia.*[13] But it is not profound or even helpful to say that this fable's immediacy is as great as a picture's when the portrait of Elisa in "April" and the fable in "May" are not granted similar praise. Also, what does the picture set before our eyes look like? —surely not like the woodcut that appears in the *Calender!* E. K. accepts the metaphors of *ut pictura poesis* uncritically, and he employs them merely to describe a general effect of immediacy that is supposed to arise from Spenser's iconic image of the oak and the briar. Twelve years later, in 1591, John Harington declares in "An Advertisement to the Reader," prefatory to his illustrated translation of the *Orlando furioso,* that "the use of the picture is euident, which is, that (hauing read ouer the booke) you may read it (as it were againe) in the very picture."[14] That you can "read" these pictures as a mnemonic is partly true: the illustration to canto 1, for example, shows Rinaldo six times with his name inscribed near each image; but Ariosto's interlacing of events is no more than roughly apparent in this engraving, even though Sacripante does seem to go off with Angelica in the end (i.e., at the top). This attempt to find a spatial equivalent for narrative movement

---

shown that the first Renaissance treatise on painting, Alberti's *Della pittura,* takes its rhetorical organization from Ciceronian rhetoric, and goes far in the direction of identifying the aims and means of painting with those of rhetoric: "In both cases the educative role is of the greatest importance and in both it is concealed from the audience" (p. 26).

[13] *Variorum,* 7.255-256; also Hagstrum, p. 63.

[14] *Orlando Fvrioso in English Heroical Verse* (London, 1591), sig. A1 recto.

leaves even the well-informed reader to seek assistance from labels and to ask if pictures really are silent poems.

Although *ut pictura poesis* became a dogma of Renaissance criticism, one major literary critic, Lodovico Castelvetro, dissented. He found significant differences between the arts of painting and poetry, and many of his ideas anticipate the attack upon the doctrine in the eighteenth century.[15] Quite atypically for his time, Castelvetro says that painting differs from poetry not only in its means but also in its objects of imitation. A painting is admired for faithfully representing real things. We admire poems for representing, as if they were real, things which are unreal but probable inventions. Painting is a literal art, but poetry is an imaginative one.[16] Further, painting is best at showing objects, whereas poetry represents human actions and thoughts. Finally, history painting and the human actions it attempts to represent are not at all the proper concern of painters: "What in poetry is first, taken most into account, and esteemed the most—the proper imitation of

---

[15] See Lodovico Castelvetro, *Poetica d'Aristotele vulgarizzata et sposta* (Basel, 1576), pp. 41, 72-74, 342, 586; Bernard Weinberg, "Castelvetro's Theory of Poetics," in *Critics and Criticism*, ed. R. S. Crane (Chicago, 1952), p. 369; H. B. Charlton, *Castelvetro's Theory of Poetry* (Manchester, 1913), pp. 16-17, 35-38, 62-65; Hagstrum, p. 61, n. 19 and p. 65, n. 28; and Andrew Bongiorno, "Castelvetro's Commentary on the *Poetics* of Aristotle," Diss. Cornell 1935, pp. 126-131.

[16] Castelvetro's idea of painting is none too sympathetic. For example: "The painting of a monster which has never existed and which we have never seen or heard or had any knowledge of in any other way gives us none of the pleasure which is properly derived from an imitation; but it may give us pleasure of another kind. Examples of this type of painting are certain canvases painted in Flanders. In like manner a poem which tells some fantastic story that has never happened, and cannot or is unlikely to happen, gives us none of the pleasure properly derived from an imitation, though it may give pleasure by its other elements, such as the purity of its diction, the beauty of its figures, or the music of its verse." *Poetica d'Aristotele vulgarizzata*, pp. 73-74 (Bongiorno translation, p. 130).

Ut Pictura Poesis *and Imagery*

human action—is the last in painting and of no account at all; that is, what the painters call history. . . . And what is rejected in poetry—the imitation of reality—. . . not only is not rejected in painting, it is praised."[17] Here Castelvetro anticipates things to come.

The first full-scale attack on the reigning dogma of *ut pictura poesis* occurred in 1766, when Lessing published his famous *Laokoön*.[18] In the preface Lessing insists that the

[17] *Poetica d'Aristotele vulgarizzata,* p. 586 (author's translation).

[18] That the fundamental ideas in Lessing's treatise were not entirely original has been widely observed. Leonardo, with an opposite bias, made some similar arguments in the Renaissance: see Jean P. Richter and Irma A. Richter, *The Literary Works of Leonardo da Vinci* (Oxford, 1939), I, 3-56; Giuseppina Fumagalli ed., *Leonardo: omo sanza lettere* (Florence, 1952), pp. 238-248. Predecessors of Lessing in eighteenth-century England were the "Discourse on Music, Painting and Poetry" by James Harris in *Three Treatises* (London, 1744), and Edmund Burke, *A Philosophical Enquiry into the Origin of Our Ideas of the Sublime and Beautiful* (London, 1757); in France, Diderot's *Lettre sur les sourds et les muets* (Paris, 1751), appeared and was reviewed by Lessing. On these predecessors and others see Dorothy Reich, ed., *Laokoön* (Oxford, 1965), pp. 29-32; Hagstrum, pp. 151-153; René Wellek, *A History of Modern Criticism: 1750-1950*, I (New Haven, 1955), 159-167; and, for further references, E. H. Gombrich, "Lessing (Lecture on a Master Mind)," *Proceedings of the British Academy*, XLIII (1957), 138, n. 5. Wellek dismisses these as scattered anticipations and gives Lessing the palm for striking and persuasive formulation. Gombrich, p. 139, on the other hand, says the basic distinction was "commonplace in eighteenth-century critical literature," and is discontented that the *Laokoön* should "owe its fame only to the brilliant presentation of an idea which was neither new nor, as it happens, quite correct." He sees Lessing as a defender of the natural-sublime against the domination of French classicism in Germany; the main attack of the *Laokoön* is aimed at Winckelmann because his discovery and adulation of "the noble simplicity and majestic calm of Greek statuary" was seen by Lessing as support for the cold rigors of French literature (p. 143). Gombrich says that "in the *Laocoön* Lessing erects a high fence along the frontiers between art and literature to confine the fashion of neo-classicism within the taste for the visual arts, where indeed it remained unchallenged till Fuseli discovered the pictorial equivalent to Shakespeare in the rude sublimities of Rembrandt" (p.

Introduction

ancients recognized the metaphorical character of the parallel
between painting and poetry; he reasserts the Aristotelian
distinction among the arts according to the *means* of imitation,
and he distinguishes proper *objects* of imitation for each art.
His theoretical description of the arts found in Chapter xvi
assumes that the means and the object of artistic imitation
should stand in a direct, logical relationship to one another:
"If it is true that in its imitations painting uses completely
different means or signs than does poetry, namely figures and
colors in space rather than articulated sounds in time, and if
these signs must indisputably bear a suitable relation to the
thing signified, then signs existing in space can express only
objects whose wholes or parts coexist, while signs that follow
one another can express only objects whose wholes or parts
are consecutive."[19] Lessing would confine painting to the
representation of objects in space, poetry to the narration of
progressive actions; he rejects works of art in which "signs"
are not suitably related to the "things signified." Still, he does
not presume that visual perception is absolutely atemporal or
that language is incapable of representing objects in space. We
perceive an object in space, he says, by seeing its parts in their
relation to one another and then conceiving the object as a
whole so quickly that the process seems instantaneous. Even
if the poet could imitate this process exactly, the beginning of
his account would be forgotten before he reached the end.[20]

For all of these reasons, Lessing thinks that descriptive
poetry is not properly poetic. He believes that poetry should

---

144). Gombrich's account is persuasive, but Lessing's treatise has been
very influential, and is the best known of the attacks on *ut pictura
poesis*.

[19] *Laokoön*, Dorothy Reich, ed. (Oxford, 1965), p. 157. The transla-
tion quoted in my text is by Edward A. McCormick (New York, 1962),
p. 78.

[20] *Laokoön*, Chapter xvii, p. 166. McCormick, pp. 85-86.

14

be illusionistic, but that extended description works against that immediacy upon which true verisimilitude depends:[21] "I do not deny to language altogether the power of depicting the corporeal whole according to its parts. It can do so because its signs, although consecutive, are still arbitrary. But I do deny it to language as the medium of poetry, because the illusion, which is the principal object of poetry, is wanting in such verbal description of bodies .... the coexistent nature of a body comes into conflict with the consecutive nature of language, and although dissolving the former into the latter makes the division of the whole into its parts easier for us, the final reassembling of the parts into a whole is made extremely difficult and often even impossible."[22]

Lessing's assertion that poetry is properly an art of time and narration whereas painting is an art of space and description supports his attack upon the excessive, often merely enumerative, description in eighteenth-century poetry. Details no doubt are lost to the reader by the conclusion of an elaborate description, but Lessing's analogy between the procedure of such poetry and the process of visual perception is misleading. Extended description fails in poetry not merely because its massing of detail is slower than the eye's instantaneous cataloging of everything in view. The eye is quick, but it cannot catalog every detail of the visible world. Modern research indicates that visual perception, no less than the aural comprehension of poetry, is a process in time which depends very much upon conventional signs, systems of understanding, cues, and as-

[21] See Hagstrum, pp. 134-140, on the principle of *enargeia* in the eighteenth century, and, pp. 155-156, on those elements of Lessing's theory that are consistent with the doctrines of *ut pictura poesis*.

[22] *Laokoön*, Chapter XVII, p. 169. McCormick, p. 88. In this passage Lessing refers to the distinction between natural signs (images) and conventional signs (language). According to E. H. Gombrich, *Art and Illusion*, 2nd ed. (Princeton, 1961), pp. 87 and 360-362, Plato's *Cratylus* is the first major statement of this distinction.

sumptions, not upon instantaneous perception of natural signs. The poet's challenge is to control visual detail and to find its significance, as our perceptual systems do, without being overcome by it—but this, broadly speaking, is my subject.

Neither Lessing's strictures nor the later hostility in major romantic criticism toward eighteenth-century ideas of *ut pictura poesis* seems to have affected the cataloging of that gallery of pictures that Alexander Pope, like Spence's aged mother, envisioned in Spenser.[23] Many distinguished writers have concluded from their impression of pictorialism in Spenser's poetry that comparisons with specific paintings or painters would be instructive, and many have contributed to the master catalog of the Spenserian gallery. Hippolyte Taine, writing in his *History of English Literature*, is a particularly eloquent example. He makes the same metaphorical identification of invention with design that we have already observed in Dryden's "Parallel":

> Spenser's characteristic is the vastness and the overflow of picturesque invention. Like Rubens, he creates whole scenes, beyond the region of all traditions, to express distinct ideas. As with Rubens, his allegory swells its proportions beyond all rule, and withdraws fancy from all law, except in so far as it is necessary to harmonise forms and colours. . . . We

---

[23] Joseph Spence, *Observations, Anecdotes, and Characters*, ed. J. M. Osborn (Oxford, 1966), I, 182. On the metaphor's history see M. H. Abrams, *The Mirror and the Lamp* (New York, 1953), pp. 48-56, especially p. 50: "The use of painting to illuminate the essential character of poetry—*ut pictura poesis*—so widespread in the eighteenth century, almost disappears in the major criticism of the romantic period; the comparisons between poetry and painting that survive are casual. . . ." See, also, Hagstrum, p. 151: "Burke and Lessing may have contributed to the virtual disappearance of *ut pictura poesis* in major romantic criticism and to the replacement of painting by music as the art most analogous to poetry." These assertions are significantly modified by Roy Park, " '*Ut Pictura Poesis*': The Nineteenth-Century Aftermath," *JAAC*, xxviii (1969), 155-164.

find here finished pictures, genuine and complete, composed
with a painter's feeling, with choice of tints and lines; our
eyes are delighted by it. This reclining Acrasia has the pose
of a goddess, or of one of Titian's courtesans. An Italian
artist might copy these gardens, flowing waters, sculptured
loves, wreathes of creeping ivy thick with glossy leaves and
fleecy flowers. Just before, in the infernal depths, the lights
with their long streaming rays, were fine, half-smothered by
the darkness; the lofty throne in the vast hall . . . connected
all the forms around it by centring all regards. The poet,
here and throughout, is a colourist and an architect.[24]

Even before the nineteenth century there were many charming
but indiscriminate and impressionistic comparisons of Spenser
with painters, and the influence of this tradition is strong even
today. Of course both Rubens and Titian have rooms in the
Spenserian gallery, but over the years the collection has grown
to include nearly every major European painter. It is pointless
to list them here, for, as one scholar says, such criticism varies
chiefly with the quality of the writer's course in the history
of art.[25]

[24] H. A. Taine, *History of English Literature*, trans. H. van Laun
(New York, 1879), pp. 195 and 199.
[25] Rudolf Gottfried, "The Pictorial Element in Spenser's Poetry,"
ELH, xix (1952), 203-213; also reprinted in *That Soueraine Light*,
ed. William R. Mueller and Don Cameron Allen (Baltimore, 1952), pp.
123-133. Gottfried mentions many critics in this tradition, including
the familiar figure of Pope's old lady, Joseph Warton, Leigh Hunt,
and Taine, as well as Edward Dowden, Jefferson B. Fletcher, and
W. L. Renwick. He takes W.B.C. Watkins's essay, "Spenser's Palace of
Art," in *Shakespeare and Spenser* (Princeton, 1950), pp. 223-258, to be
the most recent and sophisticated of the group; it has much in com-
mon with impressionistic criticism, but it also contains the seed of a
new approach to the problem and will receive special consideration
below.
An excellent introduction to the problems of comparative studies is
René Wellek, "The Parallelism between Literature and the Arts,"
English Institute Annual, 1941 (New York, 1942), pp. 29-63. Giovanni

Introduction

Most impressionistic criticism comparing poetry with paintings is harmless enough. It usually has no theoretical basis and it tends to ignore the significance of images; it is limited at best, but it still can make us notice new things. However, the recent critical fashion of using technical language from art history to describe poetic styles, including Spenser's, is far more confusing and misleading than parallels that quite openly rely upon similarity of mood or subject. The technical terms are frequently drawn from a formal system originally devised by Heinrich Wölfflin to describe the differences between Renaissance and Baroque styles in the visual arts.[26] Such terms

---

Giovannini has already described the errors of earlier studies of periods and individual authors; most of these works are in the same tradition as those, specifically on Spenser, discussed by Gottfried. Giovannini, p. 192, says that there are many indications "that comparative analysis has not advanced much since Spence's *Polymetis* and the arbitrary analogizing like that of Haydon [*Lectures on Painting and Design* (London, 1844-46)], who described the Elgin marbles as 'essentially Shakesperian.' In the studies of Manwaring [*Italian Landscape in Eighteenth Century England* (New York, 1925)], Hussey [*The Picturesque* (London, 1927)], Binyon [*Landscape in English Art and Poetry*], Tinker [*Painter and Poet* (Cambridge, Mass., 1939)], and Larrabee [*English Bards and Grecian Marbles* (New York, 1943)], terms like chiaroscuro, Claudian, sculpturesque, high coloring, when applied to literary art are largely emptied of their technical significance in the visual arts and are often confined to description of general similarity in content. While the assimilation of the terminology of the visual arts is theoretically justified, in practice the terminology, which has a precise sense in the visual arts, has paradoxically resulted in impressionism and inconsistency." Other studies which depend heavily upon similarity of content include Arthur H. R. Fairchild, *Shakespeare and the Arts of Design*, University of Missouri Studies, XII (Columbia, Mo., 1937), and Henry Green, *Shakespeare and the Emblem Writers* (London, 1870). See also, *Variorum*, 3.392-399, "Spenser's Use of the Plastic Arts."

[26] *Principles of Art History*, trans. M. D. Hottinger (New York: Dover Publications, n.d.). Wylie Sypher, *Four Stages of Renaissance Style* (Garden City, N.Y., 1955) is well known for his application of Wölfflin's terms to literary works; he treats Spenser at some length,

Ut Pictura Poesis *and Imagery*

are commonly used in art criticism. In literary criticism, although these categories may appear to be used systematically and to be based upon reputable stylistic distinctions, they operate only as general metaphors. They have been popularized and abused, yet in careful use sweeping terms like "Baroque" can describe demonstrable stylistic traits in painting and sculpture. They have usually meant little as descriptions of literary style. No literary vocabulary has been developed to support them in the way such elementary terms as Wölfflin's "linear" and "painterly" support their application in the visual arts. As Rosemond Tuve says, when they are applied to literature, terms like "Baroque" and "Mannerist" are not dependent upon "the presence of any isolatable verbal device such as the rhetorician can describe, and most tangle with difficulties raised by the inescapable conceptual dimension of words. From this attribute of the medium arises the fact that an author can control the relevance, more surely than the form, of the images we make."[27] Tuve, like René Wellek and Giovanni Giovannini before her, is calling for more self-conscious criticism, and she is insisting with them upon some attempt to

---

pp. 87-94, *et passim*. For a discussion of the validity of extensions of Wölfflin's scheme, see René Wellek, "The Parallelism between Literature and the Arts." The number of literary studies based on Wölfflin's work is vast, and grows continually. At its best, such criticism can be helpful, but its success usually depends more on discoveries made by traditional methods than upon the invocation of Wölfflin's categories. For example, in Morris W. Croll's brilliant articles on the Baroque style in prose, now published as *Style, Rhetoric, and Rhythm*, ed. J. Max Patrick, *et al.* (Princeton, 1966), Wölfflin's categories are invoked for purposes of illustration, but as Wellek says, "no far-reaching conclusion or speculations are tied to these remarks" (p. 45). Recently, Rosemond Tuve, "Baroque and Mannerist Milton?" *Milton Studies in Honor of H. F. Fletcher* (Urbana, 1961), pp. 209-225, has attempted to sweep away some of the confusion that has arisen in the attempts to apply stylistic terms taken from the history of art to Milton's style.
[27] "Baroque and Mannerist Milton?" p. 211.

define basic terms which do not obscure the great difficulties that arise in comparative studies. Terminology has changed from time to time, but there have been few real advances. Critics of Spenser, like most other students of pictorialism in literature, have continued in the tradition of *ut pictura poesis* impressionism or have combated it with arguments similar to Lessing's.

In recent writings on Spenser there have been specific attempts to deny the traditional view that he is one of the most pictorial of poets, and to reconsider—indeed to reformulate—the entire question of what Spenser's imagery is like.[28] For many modern readers the notion of pictorial imagery in Spenser is suspect because it seems too closely connected with old-fashioned appreciations of *The Faerie Queene* as a mindlessly rigid and simple moral allegory decorated with beautiful images meant to be enjoyed for themselves. Probably the greatest accomplishment of recent studies of Spenser has been to show that his images are not merely decorative, but that they are integral to the allegory. They are part of a complex metaphorical system the effect of which depends upon rhetorical arrangement of language and upon iconography, or *meaning* in the broadest sense.

Most informed readers would now agree that imagery and conceptual substance are inseparable in Renaissance poetry—certainly in Spenser—and no critic has been more influential in establishing this view than Rosemond Tuve. Her argument is wisely balanced: on the one hand, poetic "imitation" in the Renaissance was chiefly preoccupied with rendering the intelligible world as seen through the visible; on the other, the

---

[28] See especially Rudolf Gottfried, "The Pictorial Element in Spenser's Poetry," *ELH*, xix (1952), 203-213; Lyle Glazier, "The Nature of Spenser's Imagery," *MLQ*, xvi (1955), 300-310; Carl Robinson Sonn, "Spenser's Imagery," *ELH*, xxvi (1959), 156-170; and Paul J. Alpers, "Narrative and Rhetoric in the *Faerie Queene*," *SEL*, ii (1962), 27-46.

visible world remained an immediate object of imitation, and
representing it accurately was an important means to powerful
images.[29] If, indeed, we think the intelligible world to be ap-
prehended through the external or sensible, surely imitation of
the visible world is a way of apprehending the intelligible.
It would be difficult for a poet to pursue two such intimately
related goals without pursuing them both. As Tuve says, the co-
operative interplay between statement and image in Spenser as
in any of the greater Renaissance poets is subtle; and Spenser's
"painting" can at any moment slip "onto the level of general-
ized abstraction, where response to it draws on the reader's
fund of experience, not on his pictorial imagination. But no
greater violence to the *poetry* of Spenser could be done than,
by separating the two, to turn the poem into one vast picture
gallery."[30]

I would modify Tuve's assertions only by suggesting that
her antithesis between significant images based on experience
and pictorial images or "word-painting" is misleading. It re-

[29] *Elizabethan and Metaphysical Imagery*, pp. 33-36 and p. 56. See also
Chapter Three, "Ut Pictura Poesis."
[30] *Ibid.*, p. 59. It is worth noting that Spenser was, for an Englishman
of his time, in a position to become relatively informed about the
visual arts of his own day and of the past—both in England and on
the Continent. But, as Roy C. Strong says, "Collecting as we under-
stand it did not exist in Elizabethan England"; see *The English Icon*
(London and New York, 1969), pp. 43-50, "Collectors and Col-
lecting." Rosemond Tuve, "Spenser and Some Pictorial Conventions,"
SP, xxxvii (1940), 149-176, has pointed to dozens of possible con-
nections Spenser might have had with collectors and amateurs of
medieval books and illuminated manuscripts. Among many places
where Spenser might have been exposed to foreign works of art, the
foremost are at Court and in the collection of his patron the Earl of
Leicester: see W. A. Shaw, ed. *Three Inventories of the Years 1542,
1547 and 1549-50 of Pictures in the Collections of Henry VIII and
Edward VI* (London, 1937); Oliver Millar, *The Tudor, Stuart, and
Early Georgian Pictures in the Collection of Her Majesty the Queen*,
2 vols. (London, 1963); William J. Thoms, "Pictures of the Great Earl
of Leicester," *NQ*, 3rd ser., II (1862), 201-202 and 224-226.

turns us to Lessing's idea that words, in their proper function, have little to do with pictures and are capable of far more sophisticated psychological effects than visual imagery: that word pictures somehow limit poetry and violate its true nature. In the absence of any theory of literary pictorialism, such an antithesis is possible because pictorial imagery is so often wrongly associated with instantaneously perceived optical illusion. Spenser does not often sustain optical illusions in his poetry, but it does not follow that his imagery is unpictorial. Not all objects that we call "pictures" produce optical illusions, and even our visual comprehension of illusionistic pictures now appears to depend upon established expectations and categories in our minds. We perceive works of art in different media differently, but the ways of the mind as it labors to classify and comprehend experience are strikingly consistent. It is likely, I think, that the ultimate coherence of many complex works of art must be understood to reside in the beholder's perception of them.[31]

Toward a Theory of Pictorialism

Lessing's dichotomy between arts of time and arts of space— between succession, action, and meaning as opposed to simultaneity, stasis, and sensation—has, according to E. H. Gom-

---

[31] A similar idea is central to Paul J. Alpers' argument first in "Narrative and Rhetoric in the *Faerie Queene*," and then in *The Poetry of The Faerie Queene*. Alpers, as I understand him, advocates an affective approach to *The Faerie Queene*. He argues that the poem's internal order is not formal or narrative in any usual sense but rhetorical, and that the poet's attention is not focused on what is happening within his fiction but on the reader's mind and feelings. In my own attempts to analyze Spenser's pictorialism psychologically, I am much indebted to Alpers' conception of *The Faerie Queene*. Yet there appears to be a point of direct conflict between us: when Alpers discusses the traditional approach to Spenser's pictorialism as an example of how critical concern for fictional consistency has overridden rhetorical consideration of the poetry, he says that Spenser uses pictorial effects "to achieve a certain psychological impact, not because he wants to

brich, "remained unquestioned in aesthetics" yet has proved "barren and misleading" to critics of the arts.[32] In studies of literary pictorialism, this dichotomy has too often been an explicit or implicit premise. I wish to abandon awkward categorical distinctions between visual and literary arts, and to base my consideration of Spenser's pictorialism directly upon analysis of his literary presentation of visual materials.

It is most probably true that our understanding of visual as well as verbal signs is conventional rather than natural and universal. But the fact remains that those signs which represent the visible world in painting are visually perceived, as is the world they attempt to represent, whereas the relationship between language and visible object in poetry is more distant. Certain conventions of representation separate the most naturalistic art from nature. Pictorialism in poetry must inevitably be still more stylized and less easily confounded with ordinary vision. Therefore I do not propose purely formal identities or correspondences between works of art and of literature. I propose instead an affective and psychological approach to the problem of defining literary pictorialism. We must ask how words can be selected and organized to *imitate* the process of visual perception, not how paintings as such can be made of

---

render real visual experience" (*The Poetry of The Faerie Queene*, p. 10; also, pp. 9-14, pp. 103-105, *et passim*). Spenser certainly controls the "psychological impact" of his poetry through "our experience of words and their poetic disposition" (p. 10), but must this prevent him from rendering visual experience? The psychological impact of great paintings is often said to stem from the artist's subtle and precise control of visual perception. In Alpers' terms poetry that I would call purely "descriptive" attempts to "render real visual experience" (p. 10n.); Dante, Ariosto, and Tasso excel in it (p. 105). Such poetry in my opinion details things that we might see; unlike the writing that I term "pictorial" it ordinarily does not imitate the process of visualization. Alpers' terms differ confusingly from mine, but I do not think that we disagree sharply.

[32] "Moment and Movement in Art," *JWCI*, xxvii (1964), 295 and 300.

words. Poetry is not formally like painting, but can it create similar effects through peculiarly verbal means of imitation? Must we assume, a priori, that two kinds of imitation which produce similar effects will be identical in form? Let us grant the differences between media in the arts, and say simply that poetry is pictorial not when its formal organization reminds us of a painting or drawing, but when its relationship to our experience of the visual world is analogous to the relationship of the visual arts to that world. We must try to account for the apparent fact that the effect of reading poetry can seem like the effect of seeing these formal analogues of the visual world called pictures. The power of particular literary works to inspire actual paintings or to remind us of pictures we have seen is not in question here, nor is it very important since the quality of reminiscence and the specific pictures called to mind will always depend upon the reader's familiarity with works of art and his visual memory. The fascinating question is not what great paintings a particular poem evokes, but how poems which attempt to imitate our experience of real and imagined visual worlds can seem like pictures at all.

Many of the most important principles governing my discussion of literary pictorialism are presented with exemplary clarity and originality in two works by E. H. Gombrich, "Moment and Movement in Art" and *Art and Illusion*.[33] Gombrich argues that our ability to interpret any sort of experience in the world depends in large part upon the schemata we have learned for the classification and interpretation of experience. This is no less true in criticism than in the perception of the visible world, and it is impossible to overestimate the importance of these studies in providing new ways of asking questions about pictorialism in poetry. This is not to say that I am always faithful to his subtle distinctions, or

[33] 2nd ed., revised (Princeton, 1961). First published, 1959.

that I do not eventually stray far from the path that he started me on. Here, as a preface to the following chapters, it is possible to trace only the broad outlines of Gombrich's extraordinary work.

In "Moment and Movement in Art," Gombrich poses some new questions about the problem of the passage of time in paintings. He takes as examples of the traditional formulation of the problem Lord Shaftesbury's discussion of the Judgment of Hercules and the "Discourse on Music, Painting and Poetry" (1744) by James Harris.[34] These English precursors of Lessing present the basic notion that, because of its medium, every picture is " 'of necessity a *punctum temporis* or instant.' "[35] Gombrich submits that we "beg the most important question when we ask what 'really happens' at any point of time." He points first to the logical absurdity of this idea, for "as soon as we assume that there is a fraction of time in which there is no movement, movement as such becomes inexplicable [Zeno's paradox]" (p. 297). But the notion is more absurd psychologically: our perceptual apparatus is slow, but its very slowness creates from the flux of time "a meaningful pattern through the miracle of persistence and memory" (p. 298). If our perceptions were too fast, and we perceived only the present, television, for example, would be to us only the movement of a meaningless flickering dot. Gombrich points out that St. Augustine meditated on the fact of the elusive present's existence in our minds along with the vivid memory of the immediate past and anticipation of the immediate future (*Confessions*, XI, 27-28). He refers to modern psychologists who distinguish by experiment two distinct kinds of

[34] See *Characteristicks of Men, Manners, Opinions, Times* (London, 1714), Chapter I, "A notion of the Historical Draught, or Tablature of the Judgment of Hercules"; and James Harris, *Three Treatises*.

[35] Harris, quoted by Gombrich, "Moment and Movement in Art," p. 294.

25

memory (apart from the brief physiological persistence of a sense impression): 1) the primary or immediate memory in which "our impressions remain available for a brief span of time"[36] and which makes possible our perception of music, television, and movies; 2) the permanent and less immediate memory.

The results of modern experiments, as well as Gombrich's speculations upon them, "corrode the sharp *a priori* distinction between the perception of time and of space. Successive impressions do in fact persist *together* and are not wholly experienced as successive" (pp. 299-300). Experiments, as well as common phenomena such as spoonerisms also confirm St. Augustine's observation that while he recites one line of a psalm, his mind is anticipating the future and preparing for the recital of lines to come. All of these observations indicate that music and poetry cannot be exclusively arts of succession, and that the *punctum temporis* is equally meaningless for the painter. Gombrich reminds us that visual perception is a fairly slow process in time, and that "the reading of a picture . . . needs a very long time. There are examples in psychological literature of the weird descriptions given by people of identical paintings flashed on to a screen for as long as two seconds.[37] It takes more time to sort a painting out. . . . Photographs of eye movements suggest that the way the eye probes and gropes for meaning differs vastly from the idea of the critics who write on the artist 'leading the eye' here or there" (p. 301).[38]

[36] "Moment and Movement in Art," p. 299. Gombrich cites D. O. Hebb, *The Organization of Behavior* (New York, 1949), pp. 61-62; see also James J. Gibson, *The Perception of the Visual World* (Boston, 1950), pp. 158-159.

[37] Gombrich cites F. C. Bartlett, *Remembering* (Cambridge, Mass., 1932), pp. 29ff.; M. D. Vernon, *A Further Study of Visual Perception* (London, 1952), Appendix B.

[38] Gombrich cites Gibson, *The Perception of the Visual World*, p. 155; see also, Guy T. Buswell, *How People Look at Pictures* (Chicago, 1935).

Normally, when we look at a picture, or indeed anything in the visible world, "we build it up in time and hold the bits and pieces we scan in readiness till they fall into place as an imaginable object or event, and it is this totality we perceive and check against the picture in front of us." We are led "to a scanning backward and forward in time and in space," and to "the assignment of what might be called the appropriate serial orders which alone give coherence to the image" (p. 302).

These last paragraphs are only a brief condensation of remarks upon which Gombrich bases an analysis, influential later in my argument, of how static images in painting can "arouse in us the memories and anticipations of movement" (p. 306). Since "Moment and Movement in Art" was written after *Art and Illusion* and is a logical extension of the synthesis achieved in the earlier work, the summary above touches upon some of the book's main points. It would be foolish to pretend that there is space here for an account that would do justice to *Art and Illusion*, so I shall point to only a few principles drawn from it. The work is a synthesis of knowledge drawn from many disciplines, especially from the history of art and the psychology of perception, and it approaches many awesome problems with a fresh, inquiring, and philosophical spirit. Gombrich is committed to the idea that "the world never presents a neutral picture to us; to become aware of it means to become aware of possible situations that we can try out and test for their validity" (p. 275). He shows that our perception of the visual world depends not upon the passive apprehension of inherently self-evident natural signs, but upon a continuous process of provisional interpretation, revision, and reinterpretation of ambiguous signals. The painter's evocation of the visible world depends, like visual perception, upon conventional signs—schemata developed from past experience. As Gombrich says, after a survey of modern discoveries in the psychology of perception: "Everything points to the conclusion that the phrase the 'language of art' is more than a loose metaphor, that even to describe the visible world in images we need a developed system of schemata. This conclusion rather clashes with the traditional distinction, often discussed in the eighteenth century, between spoken words which are conventional signs and painting which uses 'natural' signs to 'imitate' reality. It is a plausible distinction, but it has led to certain difficulties. If we assume, with this tradition, that natural signs can simply be copied from nature, the history of art represents a complete puzzle" (p. 87).

The history of art is, then, not the history of man's attempts to copy a self-evident and constant "nature," but the history of schemata men have used to represent their "reactions to the world" (p. 87). Because we need interpretive schemes to "get hold of the flux of experience" (p. 88), even the history of illusionistic art is a history of conventions and motifs; when the perception of the visual world becomes a matter of specific interest to the artist, as it did in Europe between the Renaissance and the twentieth century, he ceases to be satisfied with inherited schemes and conventions, and continually compares them with experience, alters them, compares them again (p. 173).

Visual perception of the world that surrounds us is a process of mediation between familiar schemata and confusing sensory data, a continuous synthesis of provisional interpretation, revision, and reinterpretation of ambiguous signals. We may take as a familiar model of this synthetic process the portrait painter's mediation between abstract form as an idea and the highly individualized forms in the world around him:

> Once he is in possession of a standard head, he can also use it as a starting point for corrections, to measure all individual deviations against it. He may first draw it on his canvas or in his mind, not in order to complete it, but to match it

against the sitter's head and enter the differences onto his schema . . . . even a wrong schema is a useful tool. . . . If seeing were a passive process, a registration of sense data by the retina as a photographic plate, it would indeed be absurd for us to need a wrong schema to arrive at a correct portrait (p. 172).

In most paintings we see only the final result of this process of correction, unless we have preparatory studies or x-rays which show the work in several stages of composition. Some artists—most notably children and "primitives" prior to the present century—rely on the minimum functional schema (p. 295); others make synthetic images of a complexity that rivals the ordinary visible world in stimulating us "to probe and anticipate, to project our expectations, and thus to build up an imaginary world of illusion" (p. 275). But only in contrived, experimental situations do human observers confuse pictures with ordinary vision (pp. 248-256). Even when the painter's schemes become capable of a remarkable illusionistic transposition of light into paint, rich in information about the visible world, they remain conventional schemes requiring a special kind of attention, not exact transcripts of nature (pp. 298-299).[39]

In my opinion, poetry is pictorial when it embodies such processes of mediation as Gombrich discusses, and the poet engages his reader's imagination through artful, inevitably contrived, analogues of vision. In pictorial writing, information about the visual world is not transmitted by simple descriptive listing of names or terms for familiar concepts and relationships, but by the author's active encounter with visual

[39] I have received help additional to Gombrich's from the following works, besides those cited in notes 37-39: M. D. Vernon, *The Psychology of Perception* (Baltimore, 1962); Rudolf Arnheim, *Art and Visual Perception* (Berkeley and Los Angeles, 1954).

phenomena as they are puzzled out, interpreted, and ordered by the mind. One of the first poets to exhibit an explicit critical understanding of the limited pictorial verisimilitude of descriptive poetry is Keats, saying to his friend John Reynolds that he "cannot write about scenery and visitings—Fancy is indeed less than a present palpable reality, but it is greater than remembrance—you would lift your eyes from Homer only to see close before you the real Isle of Tenedos.—you would rather read Homer afterwards than remember yourself." Description tends to share the faintness and disorder of ordinary memory, but a great poet can provide immutable substitutes for transitory visual experience. Keats frequently writes detailed description, but he also feels its threatening diffuseness and in a letter to his brother Tom says that "descriptions are bad at all times." Still later he declares, "For myself I hate descriptions."[40] Although he uses the word quite inclusively, Keats's only reference to "verisimilitude" not only elucidates his distaste for description but indicates his notion of its properly employed opposite. In his famous statement about Negative Capability, "that is when man is capable of being in uncertainties, Mysteries, doubts, without any irritable reaching after fact & reason," Keats is perhaps unfair to a fellow poet but accurately defines the springs of pictorialism when he goes

[40] *The Letters of John Keats*, ed. Hyder Edward Rollins, 2 vols. (Cambridge, Mass., 1958), Letter No. 96; Letters No. 91 and 199. Walter Jackson Bate, *John Keats* (Cambridge, Mass., 1963), p. 360, takes such hostile remarks to indicate Keats's increasing awareness of "how futile the attempt at mere literal description is." Ian Jack, *Keats and the Mirror of Art* (Oxford, 1967), pp. 105-116, describes Keats's interest in scenery; but notes that "in spite of its grandeur the scenery of Scotland did not answer to Keats's deepest desires" (p. 113). He calls the remark in Letter No. 91 "anomalous." Keats's ideas on description were anticipated in a strand of eighteenth-century critical thought beginning with Addison, in which poets are admired for making the reader " 'see' a picture in response to brief but precise verbal stimulus" (see Hagstrum, pp. 138-140).

on to say that "Coleridge, for instance, would let go by a fine isolated verisimilitude caught from the Penetralium of mystery, from being incapable of remaining content with half knowledge."[41] Similarly, according to Hazlitt, the reason for the absence of "gusto" in Claude's landscapes is that "they lay an equal stress on all visible impressions."[42] Description, particularly the descriptions of scenery and picturesque views *painted* by the Nature poets of the eighteenth century, was conventionally governed precisely by an obsessive "reaching after fact & reason" and by discontent with "half knowledge." Yet the reader's task as he confronts pictorial writing, like that of the beholder facing a picture and testing its imagery through tentative projections, is to participate actively in the imagination of vision. The poet cannot show everything, and may spoil things if he tries. Subject as verses are to the consecutive temporality of language, they could never present pictures as Lessing conceived them, but I hope to show that poets can imitate the process of visualization as we now understand it.

[41] Letter No. 45. The usage of "verisimilitude" in Keats's prose is tabulated in "Appendix A" of Newell F. Ford's *The Prefigurative Imagination of John Keats* (Stanford, 1951), and Chapter Eight contains a discussion of Keats's use of the word.

[42] In "On Gusto," from *The Round Table: Selected Essays of William Hazlitt*, ed. Geoffrey Keynes (London, 1934), p. 612. In his discussion of Negative Capability, Walter Jackson Bate, p. 244, refers to other remarks about Claude Lorrain from this essay.

CHAPTER TWO

Description and Pictorialism: Focusing

T he problem of diffuseness in descriptive poetry is indirectly addressed by Dr. Johnson when he observes that Pope's *Windsor Forest* shares the fault of other poems in its genre, "as the scenes, which they must exhibit successively, are all subsisting at the same time, the order in which they are shewn must by necessity be arbitrary, and more is not to be expected from the last part than from the first. The attention, therefore, which cannot be detained by suspense, must be excited by diversity."[1] The formal order that Dr. Johnson seeks is founded upon logic, or at least upon orderly association; to him visual experience seems so disjoined from the available formal categories and rhetorical modes that there can be no correlation between the form of descriptive poetry and the viewer's perceptual relationship to its subject-matter. Dr. Johnson's sense of verisimilar forms may not be as catholic as ours, but for him as well as for us the ultimate failure of descriptive poetry is a failure of coherence, and therefore of verisimilitude. The reader may broaden his learning or experience through the "diversity" of a poem, but since real scenes and landscapes are a constant threat, a poem that attempts even momentarily to substitute for visual experience must compel the attention. Indeed, the imagination's tendency to thrust even highly stylized descriptions into this competitive relationship with Nature is to some degree the artistic problem of all descriptive poetry. The poet must find

[1] *Lives of the English Poets*, ed. George Birkbeck Hill (Oxford, 1905), III, 225.

correlative forms which by their forcefulness "detain" the attention as ordinary description does not. Simple imitation leads to the formal confusion that Johnson censures. The "word-painter" who employs description in order to make a painting of his poem usually fails to create a psychological effect analogous to that of a picture. We can perhaps discover why by studying a few descriptions and contrasting them with one kind of pictorialism.

The Nature of Description

Signs and symbols are taken to be self-explanatory in description. It consists of largely unmodified names which may direct our attention to objects and phenomena in the visible world but which do not attempt to imitate, to discover, or to order our actual experience of those objects and phenomena. For this reason description lacks pictorial force. Descriptive detail accumulates without compelling the reader to a fresh visualization and reevaluation of successive images in a developing context. Keats recognizes this tendency of description to reduce and simplify experience when he refuses to catalog his experiences as a traveler, "unless perhaps I do it in the manner of the Laputan printing press—that is I put down Mountains, Rivers Lakes, dells, glens, Rocks, and Clouds, With beautiful enchanting, gothic picturesque fine, delightful, enchancting, Grand, sublime—a few Blisters &ᶜ— and now you have our journey thus far."[2] As Keats implies, description has no inherent narrative content, but a narrative or proto-narrative structure can be easily imposed upon it. It does not exclude narrative, as we might at first suppose. It can also be ordered discursively or logically. Description is formally neutral, but of course in most literature it is not formless.

[2] *The Letters of John Keats*, ed. Hyder Edward Rollins, 2 vols. (Cambridge, Mass., 1958), Letter No. 96.

Focusing

Descriptive poetry tends to reduce visual experience to simple formulas and to be encyclopedic. The crudest type, like Keats's parody of the usual traveler's letter, would be no more than a list or catalog of things that we might see. Only very simple catalogs give no more than names, and not far removed from this extreme, for example, is the following list of compliments which composes most of one sonnet in Spenser's *Amoretti*:

> For loe my loue doth in her selfe containe
>   all this worlds riches that may farre be found,
>   if Saphyres, loe her eies be Saphyres plaine,
>   if Rubies, loe hir lips be Rubies sound:
> If Pearles, hir teeth be pearles both pure and round;
>   if Yuorie, her forhead yuory weene;
>   if Gold, her locks are finest gold on ground;
>   if siluer, her faire hands are siluer sheene:
> But that which fairest is, but few behold,
>   her mind adornd with vertues manifold.
>
> (XV, 5-14)

Apparently opposite to the extreme of a random catalog, yet equally unpictorial, is the rigidly logical diagram. Close to this extreme is the almost cartographic view opening the great panorama in *Paradise Regained*:

> With that (such power was giv'n him then) he took
> The Son of God up to a Mountain high.
> It was a Mountain at whose verdant feet
> A spacious plain outstretcht in circuit wide
> Lay pleasant; from his side two rivers flow'd,
> Th'one winding, th'other straight, and left between
> Fair Champaign with less rivers intervein'd,
> Then meeting join'd thir tribute to the Sea.[3]

[3] *Complete Poems and Major Prose*, ed. Merritt Y. Hughes (New York, 1957), *PR*, III, 251-258. All references are to this edition.

Precise cartography, elaborate cataloging, apt comparisons involving visual references, massive detail. Descriptive poetry can include any of these and many other things as well; it can be wonderful, but it does not represent perceptual experience.

There are countless varieties of descriptive poetry, some of which will be illustrated later, but for now an excellent instance is Ariosto's Alcina, a famous *tour de force* of massed description. In this passage Ariosto shows his familiarity with the principle of concentration upon which one critic says "part of Spenser's pictorialism" depends: "he restrains his descriptive talents until he reaches a place where he can utterly concentrate and intensify those images that he might have been weaving into the texture of his narrative. Much of the power of the great set pieces comes from this intensification of the imagery into great, simple iconographic symbols."[4] This is true, and rightly qualified, for clustered imagery is not inevitably pictorial despite the unquestioned necessity of "descriptive talents" to pictorial effects. No matter how extensively a poet describes visual phenomena, he may depend upon forms that are too randomly, logically, or discursively arranged to allow for pictorial treatment of image clusters, definite spaces, or iconographic symbols. As we shall see, not completeness but intensity and vividness, not quantity but form and context determine pictorial effect. These limitations imply a much narrower definition of the pictorial than is implicit in Lord Chesterfield's well-known advice to his son to read Ariosto because "his painting is excellent."[5] In *Orlando furioso* Ariosto himself signals a comparison with painting at the beginning of his description of Alcina: "Di persona era tanto ben formata,/ quanto me' finger san pittori industri" ("In figure she

---

[4] Thomas P. Roche, Jr., *The Kindly Flame* (Princeton, 1964), p. 60.
[5] Quoted by Jean H. Hagstrum, *The Sister Arts* (Chicago and London, 1958), p. 130.

was as well formed as careful painters can feign at their best").[6]
The description is long, but I think it worth quoting:

> con bionda chioma lunga et annodata:
> oro non è che più risplenda e lustri.
> Spargeasi per la guancia delicata
> misto color di rose e di ligustri;
> di terso avorio era la fronte lieta,
> che lo spazio finia con giusta meta.
>
> Sotto duo negri e sottilissimi archi
> son duo negri occhi, anzi duo chiari soli,
> pietosi a riguardare, a mover parchi;
> intorno cui par ch'Amor scherzi e voli,
> e ch'indi tutta la faretra scarchi,
> e che visibilmente i cori involi:
> quindi il naso per mezzo il viso scende,
> che non truova l'Invidia ove l'emende.
>
> Sotto quel sta, quasi fra due vallette,
> la bocca sparsa di natio cinabro;
> quivi due filze son di perle elette,
> che chiude et apre un bello e dolce labro:
> quindi escon le cortesi parolette
> da render molle ogni cor rozzo e scabro;
> quivi si forma quel suave riso,
> ch'apre a sua posta in terra il paradiso.
>
> Bianca nieve è il bel collo, e 'l petto latte;
> il collo è tondo, il petto colmo e largo:
> due pome acerbe, e pur d'avorio fatte,
> vengono e van come onda al primo margo,

---

[6] *Orlando furioso,* ed. Santorre Debenedetti and Cesare Segre
(Bologna: Commissione per i Testi di Lingua, 1960), 7. 11; trans.
Allan Gilbert, 2 vols. (New York, 1954). All references are to these
editions.

quando piacevole aura il mar combatte.
Non potria l'altre parti veder Argo:
ben si può giudicar che corrisponde
a quel ch'appar di fuor quel che s'asconde.

Mostran le braccia sua misura giusta;
e la candida man spesso si vede
lunghetta alquanto e di larghezza angusta,
dove né nodo appar, né vena escede.
Si vede al fin de la persona augusta
il breve, asciutto e ritondetto piede.
Gli angelici sembianti nati in cielo
non si ponno celar sotto alcun velo.

(7.11-15)

(with blonde hair long and curling; there is no gold that
shines and sparkles more. Over her delicate cheek was
scattered a mingled color of roses and of jessamines; of
smooth ivory was her tranquil forehead, which finished
its space at the right limit.

Beneath two black and finely drawn eyebrows are two
black eyes, rather two bright suns—full of pity in gazing,
slow in moving—around which it seems that Love sports
and flies about and that thence he empties out his quiver
and openly steals away hearts; thence down the middle
of her face extended her nose, in which Envy does not
find where he may improve it.

Underneath that, as though between two valleys, is her
mouth, touched with native cinnabar; there are two rows
of choice pearls that a sweet and beautiful lip hides and
reveals; thence come out the courteous little words that
make tender every rude and churlish heart; here is fash-
ioned that sweet smile which at its pleasure opens para-
dise on earth.

White snow is her beautiful neck and her breast is milk; her neck is round and her breast high and full; two unripe apples, yet made of ivory, come and go like waves on the very marge when a soft breeze blows on the sea. Argus would not have been able to see her other parts; it can well be supposed that what is covered corresponds to what appears openly.

Her arms show their fair proportions, and her white hand, somewhat longish and of little breadth, was often seen, where neither knot appears nor vein is too large. At the end of her splendid person is seen her short slender and rounded foot. Her angelic members born in heaven cannot be concealed under any veil.)

These stanzas are laden with visual references cast especially in the figurative form that Puttenham calls "Icon": "this maner of resemblaunce is not onely performed by likening of liuely creatures one to another, but also of any other naturall thing, bearing a proportion of similitude."[7] Henry Peacham seems to link this figure specifically with the visual arts, for it "painteth out the image of a person or thing, by comparing forme with forme, qualitie with qualitie, and one likenesse with another. . . . Vnapt proportion and vnlikenesse, are faultes which may much deforme this ornament, & like as this forme of speech is a singular iewell of eloquence, so ought the vus thereof to be very rare."[8] In the earliest edition of *The Garden of Eloquence* Peacham illustrates the figure with a sequence that could virtually be an imitation of Ariosto: "Thus I might commend by this Figure a bewtifull woman: her bodye is lyke the slender yew, her fingers lyke the whyte

[7] *The Arte of English Poesie*, ed. Gladys Doidge Willcock and Alice Walker (Cambridge, 1936), p. 244; also, pp. 241-243. Puttenham's examples indicate that the figure is not always purely visual.

[8] *The Garden of Eloqvence. . . . Corrected and Augmented by the first Author* (London, 1593), pp. 145-146.

palme braunches, that bee strypte, her eyes like glittering
pearles, her Lyppes lyke the carnation Rose, her cheekes like
the whyte Lillye, besprinckled with ruddy iuyce, her lookes
like a golden fleece."[9] Ariosto excels at such exhaustively
systematic and structured description; he begins at the top
and moves logically downward as far as he dares. The poetry
is sophisticated, witty, and tightly organized: the antithesis
"duo negri occhi, anzi duo chiari soli" refers to a tantalizing
visual paradox, but the extreme hyperbole casts it into the
realm of emblematic conceit[10] and vitiates the pictorial effect.

Ariosto's descriptions are conceived not only analytically,
but antithetically. Alcina's hair is blond but "no gold" is
brighter; her eyes are black but dazzlingly bright. An in-
genious hyperbolic image, the grotesqueness of which is con-
trolled only by an aside to correct the color, describes the form
and movement of her breasts: "due pome acerbe, e pur d'avorio
fatte,/ vengono e van come onda al primo margo,/ quando
piacevole aura il mar combatte." Strong antithetical tensions
between the ivory color and the metaphor it glosses diffuse
the immediate visual impact: "due pome acerbe" at first pre-
sents shape, color and texture, and the analytical modifier, "e
pur d'avorio fatte," which attempts to infuse the shape with
a new color and texture, cannot overcome the forcefulness of
the central metaphor. Ariosto can be precise, as he is in this
metaphor, yet his precision is more structural than phenom-
enal. The description of Alcina is a systematically organized
list of items variously adorned with simple or extremely hyper-
bolic figures. The speaker does not struggle with visual
phenomena, and once he arrives at a descriptive formula is
content (ironically or not) to offer it as a sufficient explana-
tion—Alcina's teeth are like pearls, her neck like snow, and

[9] (London, 1577), sig. U2 recto to U2 verso.
[10] I borrow this term from Frances A. Yates, "The Emblematic
Conceit in Giordano Bruno's *De Gli Eroici Furori* and in the Eliza-
bethan Sonnet Sequences," *JWCI*, vi (1943), 101-121.

her bosom like milk. Logic, wit, parody, and even cynicism are the sinews of Ariosto's descriptions, just as of his rendering of action and gesture in narrative. He seems unwilling to force us to confine our view to surfaces without anatomizing and polarizing their components and substructures. This analytical approach to mimesis is what Lodovico Dolce is admiring when he cites the description of Alcina as an "invaluable jewel" illustrating the Zeuxian method of imitation by synthesis: "In the place of *white* [bionda] Ariosto might have put *golden* locks; i.e. resembling the colour of the purest gold. This I mention, as it brings to mind what I have read in Athenaeus, that when the poets in describing Apollo use the epithet of *auricomus* (with golden locks), the painter is not to understand they mean, that the head of Apollo is to be adorned with locks of gold; nor can we suppose gold in any case proper to be introduced in painting, though frequently practised. Imitation, and the resemblances only of things, and not the introduction of the things themselves, come within the province of painting."[11] Ariosto's images have visual components, but their structure is essentially analytical and discursive, not reiterative and parallel; their shape is open, not formally closed.

A Mode of Pictorialism: Focusing

The most fundamental of the three varieties of pictorialism that I distinguish in Spenser's works occurs when real or imagined visual experience is presented in forms analogous to our most elemental processes of perception.[12] When encrusted images and metaphors accumulate around a complex visual phenomenon as the poet encounters problematic sur-

[11] *Aretino: a Dialogue on Painting* (Glasgow, 1770), pp. 113-114.
[12] For a convenient summary see M. D. Vernon, *The Psychology of Perception* (Baltimore, 1962), pp. 31-39.

faces and appearances, I shall call the resulting fixation of image "Focusing." Focused imagery divides visual experience into relatively small, intensive units the boundaries of which are defined when narration is suddenly interrupted or when it appears to retrace its course in order to deal with the same visual experience again and again. Focused imagery shapes visual materials into formal, inevitably stylized, poetic analogues of vision: embodying sights (a) themselves ambiguous or illusory, or (b) intense and perceptually complex or perplexing.

Pictorial imagery requires a special act of attention from the reader, and, as I propose to show, it differs in the treatment of its visual materials from similar imagery that requires different kinds of attention. In pictorial poetry, as distinguished from description, names or signs have to be interpreted, redefined, set apart, reshaped. In Focusing, when the poet dwells on a visual phenomenon, again and again returning to explicate it in ever more complicated attempts to provide correlative verbal terms for the experience of that phenomenon, there is an interruption of the narrative sequence, even though it may not be signalled as such. Some kind of narrative suspension is essential not only to small-scale pictorial effects, but in some degree to the larger effects to be discussed in a later chapter. In itself, however, obvious interruption of narrative is only a precondition; it alone cannot produce these effects.

Spenser's revelation of Acrasia in *The Faerie Queene* is perhaps the best illustration I know of Focused imagery— the opposite of plain description. In this passage Guyon and the Palmer, "creeping" through thickets, come upon the "display" of "That wanton Ladie, with her louer lose,/ Whose sleepie head she in her lap did soft dispose." Narration of action is excluded, and our attention is fixed with great economy of detail to a rigorously limited vision of Acrasia.

Focusing

Vpon a bed of Roses she was layd,
As faint through heat, or dight to pleasant sin,
And was arayd, or rather disarayd,
All in a vele of silke and siluer thin,
That hid no whit her alablaster skin,
But rather shewd more white, if more might bee:
More subtile web *Arachne* can not spin,
Nor the fine nets, which oft we wouen see
Of scorched deaw, do not in th'aire more lightly flee.

(2.12.77)

Spenser controls our perception of this sudden visual event
and, with characteristic amplitude, will not let us move away.
He does not describe Acrasia minutely, but provokes and
directs the imagination into an illusory sense of comprehensive
detail.

Spenser's copiousness is devoted not to a systematic inven-
tory of Acrasia's attributes, but to a fixed image. "All in a
vele of silke and siluer thin" states the subject to be developed,
and introduces the slightly hyperbolic notion of silver gather-
ing light; but the reader can organize the impression of "silke
and siluer" as he will. The next line elaborates the sensual
impression of the veil's thinness by recalling and enlarging
"disarayd," while remaining within the implications of the
original thematic statement. The declarative rhetoric of this
moment is deceptive, for "alablaster" turns out to define some-
thing neither the reader nor the viewer within the poem can
see perfectly—the whiteness of Acrasia's skin. Here Spenser
refers us to the familiar in order to define, but to define what
he both shows us directly and heightens with a veil.

The lines focus our attention on the sensuous experience
of the moment and use familiar appearances only as a starting
point. Thus, we move from a visual impression of the veil to
its magical transformation of the actual into appearance: the

ordering of Spenser's lines signals his interest in the ambiguity of appearances when he says that the veil "hid no whit her alablaster skin,/ But rather shewd more white, if more might bee." The sensuous effect is enhanced because we move from the perception of the veil to the perception of the veil over "alablaster skin," and then to a comparison between what is perceived and what is imagined to be the fact behind the veil. The effect of visual flux and complexity is intensified as the imagination alternates between different impressions of a single sight. The garment almost becomes part of the body.[13] The function of the veil is ambiguous, since it both "hid no whit" and "shewd more white": heightening, after all, can be a mode of concealment as well as of revelation.

Spenser still will not move away, but fixes upon the sparkling thinness and whiteness yet again; in the last three lines, the visual and intellectual aspects of the verse are fused as the ominous and magical connotations of something weblike are enlarged. "Nets" reiterates this idea and adumbrates the slightly later parallel of Acrasia and Verdant with Venus and Mars in Vulcan's net. The final image completes the evanescent visual impression of the veil by reducing it to light sparkling in beads of water as they themselves disappear. Thinness of space verges here on thinness and shortness of time—the veil is so thin that it will vanish in an instant.

A parallel passage from *Orlando furioso* might now help us to limit Focusing, as well as to illustrate still further my theoretical distinction between the descriptive and the picto-

---

[13] The grammar of lines four through seven of this stanza is ambiguous. It appears that "vele" is the subject of "shewd," and I read the passage in this way; however, it is possible that "skin" is the subject "understood from the object of a preceding verb." See Herbert W. Sugden, *The Grammar of Spenser's Faerie Queene*, Language Dissertations Published by the Linguistic Society of America, No. 22 (Philadelphia, 1936), p. 32. I do not think that the grammatical ambiguity affects my basic argument.

rial.[14] As in Spenser, the extreme sheerness of a garment is the subject and the beginning is a relatively kinesthetic image. Here is Ariosto's description of Alcina:

> ben che né gonna né faldiglia avesse;
> che venne avolta in un leggier zendado
> che sopra una camicia ella si messe,
> bianca e suttil nel più escellente grado.
> Come Ruggiero abbracciò lei, gli cesse
> il manto; e restò il vel suttile e rado,
> che non copria dinanzi né di dietro,
> più che le rose o i gigli un chiaro vetro.
>
> (7.28)

(even though she had neither gown nor hoopskirt, for she came clad in a light silk robe she had put on over a nightgown, white and sheer to the utmost extent. When Ruggiero embraced her, her robe fell off, and there remained the sheer and thin garment that did not cover her, before or behind, more than clear glass does roses or lilies.)

Ariosto's description turns on a narrative event; we know about the sheer gown, "una camicia," before it is shown, and it is only revealed by an action in the poem—Ruggiero's embrace. Likewise, the first description (almost specification) of it, "bianca e suttil nel più escellente grado," is extremely intellectual and conceptual. When the gown is described, its quality is defined by simple reference to familiar things in combination—glass, roses, and lilies. Ariosto's purpose is to present the gown conceptually as an element of narrative, not to show its appearance. He orders visual detail primarily to render action and motivation forcefully. Just prior to this

[14] Spenser's imitation of Tasso in the Bowre of Blisse is discussed in my final chapter.

stanza the dazzling Alcina has appeared to Ruggiero, who has been languishing in anticipation on perfumed sheets and is so overcome by lust that he springs up to seize her without even waiting for her to undress—"né può tanto aspettar ch'ella si spoglie" (7.27). The description of her attire hovers perfectly in the narrative, motivating the sudden embrace, showing her complicity, and supplying details of dress necessary to the next action. Ariosto's subtle *entrelacement* of visual detail to illustrate action is surely one of the most pervasive and admirable features of his art, but he also uses description to objectify action through wit. A particularly delicate variety of this device is shown by the tag, "più che le rose o i gigli un chiaro vetro," which calls up a scene of innocent nudity in Boccaccio where some ladies visiting an idyllic valley swim in a secluded lake: "il quale non altramenti li lor corpi candidi nascondeva che farebbe una vermiglia rosa un sottil vetro" (which did not hide their white bodies any more than subtle glass a red rose).[15]

Ariosto subtly embeds visible elements in a sequence of action in order to heighten its forcefulness—and as commentary. Spenser's stanza about Acrasia, on the other hand, pictorially refines an imagined visual experience through a sequence of increasingly metaphoric explanatory grids shifting over a single ineffable phenomenon. Spenser's treatment of visual materials is Focused and pictorial rather than descriptive because of an implicit recognition of the complexity of visual phenomena: he finds a rhetorical analogue that links heightened sensations of vision in Faerie Land with the world that he and the reader normally confront. In this respect his use of visual detail is parallel to Ariosto's use of wit to mediate between his highly stylized fiction and the reader's experience. The process of the stanza about Acrasia is precisely

---

[15] *Il Decameron*, ed. Charles S. Singleton, 2 vols. (Bari, 1955), II, 36. Author's translation. Charles Klopp called my attention to this parallel.

analogous to our constant perceptual struggle to comprehend visual experience by comparing it with familiar schemata from the past. These schemata define the relative chaos of perceived phenomena, just as Spenser's encrusted metaphors define the bare statement "And was arayd, or rather disarayd."

B.E.C. Davis perfectly distills the commonplace observation of Spenser's exuberant copiousness when he observes that in contrast to Chaucer, "lavish imagery, verbal or conventional as well as visual, is Spenser's natural mode of poetic utterance. He cannot dispense with figure in representing even so simple a natural phenomenon as the time of day."[16] Chaucer, on the other hand, "excels in his use of the odd and unexpected," but "formality in the design or structure of a word-portrait would be foreign to his purpose. His larger pieces . . . are catalogues of massed particulars in which he runs breathlessly from item to item, linked only by the formula 'I saw'; and even the figures of his foregrounds . . . are little more than summary sketches" (p. 161). Chaucer is the earlier English poet whose work offers the best contrast to Spenser's, at least for the present purpose of discriminating between pictorialism and related literary forms. A brief analysis of Chaucer's handling of visual materials should help to illuminate Spenser's technique.

Chaucer's is a style in which intellectual transparency combines with spareness to create the impression that the poet, though engaged with his scene, always attends thoroughly to ideas, to argument, and to structural unity. Details, including many of those that create a certain verisimilitude in the characters, lead us directly to the ideas Chaucer has in mind. He excels at creating such direct poetic correlatives for his ideas that we are convinced of the justice of his observations as well as of his wisdom. D. W. Robertson, Jr., accounts for

[16] *Edmund Spenser* (Cambridge, 1933), p. 165.

the superficial inconsistency of Chaucer's iconographic display of meaning when he observes that "details of biography, action, costume, physiognomy, and manners are sometimes mixed in what seems to be a random order. Chaucer seems unwilling to adopt a consistent 'point of view' in his descriptions so as to arrange his materials to form a coherent surface. The reason for this, however, is obvious if we remember that his interest was not in the 'surface reality' but in the reality of the idea."[17]

Of course, Spenser too is interested in the reality of ideas, but surfaces detain him and their correlation with abstractions becomes skewed. For Spenser, as Davis points out, "embellishment of a simple idea with a tissue of elaborate imagery, which no other poet has employed so successfully, is often the means of imparting new vitality to conventional figure" (p. 166). In the "Letter to Raleigh" Spenser himself describes *The Faerie Queene* as a "darke conceit," with the clear implication that the continuing metaphorical surface of his allegory, though not easily penetrated, ultimately contains abstract truth. Certainly *The Faerie Queene* abounds in personified abstractions, but it is even richer in elaborations of sensuous, and especially of visual, experience. The treatment of Acrasia's gown is but one example of Spenser's tendency to linger over the embroidery of sensuous experience. The

---

[17] *A Preface to Chaucer* (Princeton, 1962), pp. 247-248. From a slightly different perspective, Morton W. Bloomfield seems to have in view the same characteristic features of Chaucer's style when he implies a dialectic in the poet's art between a "new realism of the unreal" (Wolfgang Clemen's phrase for the early poetry) and the framed treatment of detail in *The Canterbury Tales*, which creates "a new unreality of the real so that the real could be brought into art." "Authenticating Realism and the Realism of Chaucer," *Thought*, xxxix (1964), 357. Claes Scharr, *The Golden Mirror* (Lund, 1955), quotes many of the most important descriptive passages from Chaucer. The discussion itself is not very informative.

cumulative effect of his figuration is an aura of significance, but often it is difficult to establish the cumulative meaning, or even to establish the significance of any single detail.[18] This is a partial explanation for the critical confusion surrounding most of Spenser's works. The case is somewhat similar to the "mousetrap" in the *Mérode Altarpiece* by Robert Campin (The Master of Flemalle) : most people think that the object, painted in astonishing detail, outside Joseph's window is a mousetrap, but others disagree; no one seems to be able to demonstrate what it means, even though everyone agrees that it means something.[19] Often, as with Acrasia's gown, Spenser seems fascinated with defining a complex surface, and gently confident that metaphorical refraction will automatically cause it to yield up its meaning. A poet in the Middle Ages, as Phillip Damon says, theoretically "does not transform, transvalue or otherwise modify the things he selects from the world as objectively given. With minor exceptions for extreme cases, they come to him with their meanings, their truth, and their beauty solidly embedded in them."[20] Spenser's use of traditional materials is often conventional, but in order to control the reader's responses he sometimes employs conflicting iconographic symbols synthetically and verges upon being anti-iconographic. Spenser's poetry is unmistakably Renaissance poetry with a medieval flavor; both the lavishness of his poetic surfaces and his fascination with human experience of the phenomenal world are its distinguishing marks.

To say that embellished and incrusted imagery is characteris-

[18] Paul J. Alpers, *The Poetry of The Faerie Queene* (Princeton, 1967), discusses some of the difficulties involved in iconographic interpretation of Spenser; see "Iconography in *The Faerie Queene*," pp. 200-234.

[19] See Irving L. Zupnick, "The Mystery of the Mérode Mousetrap," *Burlington Magazine*, cviii (1966), 126-133.

[20] "History and Idea in Renaissance Criticism," in *Literary Criticism and Historical Understanding*, ed. Phillip Damon (New York and London, 1967), p. 33.

tic of Spenser is not to deny that certain passages in *The Faerie Queene* display the apparent randomness of a catalog. A well-known example is the list of trees in the forest where Errour lurks (1.1.8-9), a passage with many sources and analogues; *The Parliament of Fowls* appears to be the chief source, with Ovid standing in the background.[21] Spenser's list is longer than Chaucer's, and there is perhaps more variety in the structure of his lines, but the two catalogs have the same rambling structure. Other similarities, which paradoxically serve to heighten the contrast between the two poets, include the use of personified abstractions and a tendency to place action before a neutral background or against a few iconographically conceived details of setting. Much of what Robertson says about the spatial incoherence of such settings in Chaucer, even when "like the painted chamber with its stained-glass windows in *The Book of the Duchess*" they appear to resemble "locations actually observed," is also true of Spenser: "The framework of *The Canterbury Tales* exhibits a typical Gothic disregard for spatial coherence. . . . Beyond a few references to place-names no details of the scene are given. . . . The pilgrims might just as well be seen moving against a background of gold leaf."[22] In *The Faerie Queene* too there are only the most isolated links to a coherent geography. The archaic flavor of Spenser's narrative is compounded of more than his nostalgic obsession with antique times, romance materials, and

[21] See *Variorum*, 1.179-182, and *The Works of Geoffrey Chaucer*, 2nd ed., F. N. Robinson, ed. (Cambridge, Mass., 1957), ll.172-182. All references are to this edition.

[22] *A Preface*, p. 258. These observations on Chaucer recall Coleridge's on Spenser: "You will take especial note of the marvellous independence and true imaginative absence of all particular space or time in the Faery Queene. It is in the domains neither of history or geography; it is ignorant of all artificial boundary, all material obstacles; it is truly in land of Faery, that is, of mental space." *Coleridge's Miscellaneous Criticism*, ed. Thomas Middleton Raysor (Cambridge, Mass., 1936), p. 36.

a few obsolete words; the spacelessness of the poem contributes forcefully to the pervasive archaism of its atmosphere.

The lines describing Alceste as she appears with Cupid in the "Prologue" of *The Legend of Good Women* are a particularly useful illustration of the differences between Spenser's and Chaucer's use of visual materials:

> And from afer com walkyng in the mede
> The god of Love, and in his hand a quene,
> And she was clad in real habit grene.
> A fret of gold she hadde next her heer,
> And upon that a whit corowne she beer
> With flourouns smale, and I shal nat lye;
> For al the world, ryght as a dayesye
> Yecrouned ys with white leves lyte,
> So were the flowrouns of hire coroune white.
> For of o perle fyn, oriental,
> Hire white coroune was ymaked al;
> For which the white coroune above the grene
> Made hire lyk a daysie for to sene,
> Considered eke hir fret of gold above.
>
> (Text F, 11, 212-225)

There are hints in this passage of the techniques already noted in Spenser's image of Acrasia's gown, and at first Chaucer appears to be employing the device I have called Focusing. First we learn that there is a white crown "with flourouns smale" placed over a gold net, then that the leaves are like a daisy's "white leves lyte," and then that the crown is really "of o perle fyn, oriental." There is here something of the effect produced by Spenser's shifting redefinitions of experience, but the final descriptive element is visually incongruous because the crown is conceived as a single impressive pearl. In addition, most of the descriptive terms such as colors are taken to be self-explanatory and absolute—not, as in Spenser, to be categories whose relationships to experience are confusing, surprising, or elusive. The lady is presented only as a daisy in this description, and the explanations serve only to make her iconic appearance clear.[23] In neither text of *The Legend of Good Women* is her name mentioned until well after this description; Chaucer is explaining not the sensuous, but the intellectual significance of the daisy. Even granted that there may be an element of wit in the narrator's passion for daisies, the effect is to submerge the personage so deeply within an

[23] In my use of the term "iconic," I follow the general sense set forth by Puttenham in his discussion of the figure called "Icon"— "resemblaunce by imagerie." Thus, Puttenham says, "so we commending her Maiestie for wisedome bewtie and magnanimitie likened her to the Serpent, the Lion and the Angell, because by common vsurpation, nothing is wiser then the Serpent, more couragious then the Lion, more bewtifull then the Angell," *The Arte of English Poesie*, ed. Gladys Doidge Willcock and Alice Walker (Cambridge, 1936), p. 243. See also, W. K. Wimsatt, Jr., *The Verbal Icon* (New York, 1962), p. x. Literary "icons" in this sense can be, but are not inherently, pictorial; the mere naming of the iconic figure is enough to convey its tenor to the appropriately educated reader, or in the case of pictures to the viewer. Historians of art have been the most sophisticated students of images of this kind; one of the most important and influential works in the field is Erwin Panofsky's *Studies in Iconology* (New York, 1939 and 1962). The changing significances of images have been traced, and difficult images such as personifications have also been studied. Thus, for example, the iconographer could trace through art and literature the components of an iconic figure in *The Faerie Queene*:

> The doubtfull Damzell [Una] dare not yet commit
> Her single person to their barbarous truth,
> But still *twixt feare and hope amazd does sit,*
> Late learnd what harme to hastie trust ensu'th.
> (1.6.12; italics mine)

In *The Sister Arts* (Chicago and London, 1958), Jean H. Hagstrum uses the word "iconic" to indicate "literary descriptions of works of graphic art" (p. 18, n. 34). This is a perfectly acceptable usage, but it is not widely recognized, and does not suit the purposes of my study as well as the more usual sense. I use the word "ecphrastic" to indicate literary descriptions of real or imagined works of visual art.

iconographic figure or sign that the sign is what we see. Far from dwelling upon visual phenomena, Chaucer moves almost immediately to a sign, and then assures absolute clarity by repetition. He forces us through the immediate surfaces of visual phenomena to an encounter with their significance embodied in an iconographic representation of conceptual reality.[24] The poem is a rich unfolding of significance. All of the complex implications of Alceste's wifely virtue and of her figural embodiment[25] of the Virgin Mary's aspect as partner in an ideal marriage are distilled into the image of the daisy as an iconographic representation of interwoven concepts which exist in the locus of "Alceste" as sign and "daisy" as sign.[26] The effect is complex, and the poetic which generates it is sophisticated, but brilliant as the result may be the imagery is iconic, not pictorial as the term is defined here.

Taken as a general formulation which is not intended to cover all cases, one of E. H. Gombrich's statements contrasting medieval and Renaissance art can serve the distinction

[24] *A Preface*, p. 272, *et passim.*

[25] On "figural" representation and interpretation see Eric Auerbach, " 'Figura'," pp. 11-76 in *Scenes from the Drama of European Literature* (New York, 1959). I do not at all mean to enter the complex, specialized controversy among medievalists over the question of the validity of "figural" interpretation in secular literature, nor do I mean by citing Robertson's excellent analysis of Gothic features in fourteenth-century literature to indicate unreserved acceptance of his general views.

[26] The idea of Alceste as an archetype of wifely faithfulness, who, according to Chaucer, "taught al the craft of fyn lovynge,/ And namely of wyfhod the lyvynge" (544-545), is fused with the image of a flower associated with virtue and with the Virgin Mary. Robertson says that "Alceste is . . . said to be typical of the 'holy virgin' married to God who had rather die physically in martyrdom than that her husband should die spiritually in the hearts of men" (p. 378); also that according to Deschamps, green in the daisy symbolizes *seurté*, white *purté*, and gold *sens*, and that the daisy is conventionally associated with Mary. Robertson, p. 225n., quotes from *SATF*, III, 379-380. On Alceste in particular and the question of iconic flowers in general, see *A Preface*, p. 225n. and pp. 378-379.

between descriptive and pictorial poetry: "That dry psychological formula of schema and correction can tell us a good deal, not only about the essential unity between medieval and post-medieval art, but also of their vital difference. To the Middle Ages, the schema is the image; to the postmedieval artist, it is the starting point for corrections, adjustments, adaptations, the means to probe reality and to wrestle with the particular."[27] Spenser is so striking as a pictorial poet partly because elements of both the medieval and the post-medieval exist in his work, and at least in *The Faerie Queene* are often startlingly juxtaposed.

Descriptive or Pictorial?

As I have already suggested, in the poetic handling of visual materials there can be no absolute boundaries separating the metaphoric complexity of Focusing from ordinary description. That systematic detail and ingenious comparison alone are not enough is demonstrated by Ariosto's description of Alcina; that isolated and unelaborated detail cannot create the effect we are discussing should be equally clear. For example, the sudden disclosure of Marfisa in *Orlando furioso* is an obvious, but undeveloped, occasion for elaboration:

> Al trar degli elmi, tutti vider come
> avea lor dato aiuto una donzella:
> fu conosciuta all' auree crespe chiome
> et alla faccia delicata e bella.
> L'onoran molto, e pregano che 'l nome
> di gloria degno non asconda.
>
> (26.28)

(At the pulling off of their helmets, all saw that a maiden had given them aid; she was known by her curling golden hair and her fair and tender face. They honor her much and pray her not to hide her name so worthy of glory.)

[27] *Art and Illusion*, 2nd ed. (Princeton, 1961), p. 173.

At the end of the anticipatory first clause, Ariosto's suspension of the subject in immediate juxtaposition with the stanza's few descriptive terms heightens their force, but the energy of this description is narrative in a context of rapidly related events and actions.

On a similar occasion later in *Orlando furioso* there is a burst of similes in which visual materials are prominent, but the effect of suspense when Bradamante reveals herself is still not pictorial in any of the senses I define:

> La donna, cominciando a disarmarsi,
> s'avea lo scudo e dipoi l'elmo tratto;
> quando una cuffia d'oro, in che celarsi
> soleano i capei lunghi e star di piatto,
> uscì con l'elmo; onde caderon sparsi
> giù per le spalle, e la scopriro a un tratto
> e la feron conoscer per donzella,
> non men che fiera in arme, in viso bella.
>
> Quale al cader de le cortine suole
> parer fra mille lampade la scena,
> d'archi e di più d'una superba mole,
> d'oro e di statue e di pitture piena;
> o come suol fuor de la nube il sole
> scoprir la faccia limpida e serena:
> così, l'elmo levandosi dal viso,
> mostrò la donna aprisse il paradiso.
>
> (32.79-80)

(Beginning to disarm herself, the lady had taken off her shield and then her helmet, when a coif of gold, in which her long locks were wont to be concealed and lie hidden, came off with her helmet, so they fell scattered down over her shoulders and revealed her in an instant and made her known as a woman, not less beautiful in face than terrible in arms.

Descriptive or Pictorial?

As at the falling of the curtains, amid a thousand lights
the stage appears full of arches and of more than one proud
tower and of gold and of statues and of pictures, or as the
sun reveals his clear bright face outside the clouds, so, when
she took her helmet from her face, that woman seemed
to open paradise.)

Here the sudden leap from the simple yet complete narration
of Bradamante's action to distant comparisons in the similes
excludes concrete linkage between the initial visual event and
its metaphorical elaboration. The first simile in particular
springs off so wildly and with such descriptive profusion that
it threatens to become a list before Ariosto closes it firmly with
"piena"; our pleasure in the figure, apart from its immediate
sensuous appeal, is delayed until a conceptual fusion of the
simile and its object occurs in the last three words of the
stanza. The second comparison is more immediately compre-
hensible, but not until the last line of the stanza does the poet
join it to the first simile and reveal a full burden of signifi-
cance. Ariosto's ingenuity draws attention away from the
original event to the sophisticated interpretation of action im-
plicit in his juxtaposed similes. The theatrical simile in fact
amasses dissimilarities, and the climactic arrangement of the
stanza is so eroded by its obtrusive opening that the whole is
lightly bathetic. Wit becomes the means to a precise assess-
ment of Bradamante, who may be impressive but is not, after
all, any more divine than stage architecture. Ariosto's wit, his
ironic objectivity, his skeptical poise, all are incompatible with
that visual concentration so notable in Focused imagery. He
writes perfectly conceptualized and formally controlled poetry
in which description is used illustratively; the effect is a con-
tinuous but abstracted and diffused awareness of an imagined
visual world. Ariosto tends to move directly from surfaces to
ideas about them. Spenser lingers over the surfaces themselves

and makes them seem to contain ever more significance without necessarily making that significance wholly intelligible. In the description of Bradamante's discovery, when Ariosto does seem to dwell on visual experience, he treats it with the ingenuity of an emblemist abstracting the commonplace and the esoteric into unity.

Ariosto's disclosure of Marfisa (26.28) represents an extreme of simple and visually unprovocative statement, and the previously discussed description of Alcina (7.11-15) approaches an opposite extreme of systematic description without pictorial concentration. At what point between these two extremes do we find Focused imagery and under what circumstances does it exist? Spenser's treatment of the visual elusiveness of Acrasia's gown is a firm example of Focused pictorial technique, and Ariosto's description of Bradamante illustrates multiple imagery which yet is visually diffuse. But the spectrum of possibilities is still not fully defined. Some moments of revelation in *The Faerie Queene* parallel to these from *Orlando furioso* should carry us toward an understanding of Focusing. Closer to the pictorial than Ariosto's revelation of Marfisa or Spenser's unremarked disclosure of Britomart in the Castle Joyeous (3.1.63) is the scene of Britomart's arrival in Malbecco's castle:

> And eke that straunger knight emongst the rest,
> Was for like need enforst to disaray:
> Tho whenas vailed was her loftie crest,
> Her golden locks, that were in tramels gay
> Vpbounden, did them selues adowne display,
> And raught vnto her heeles; like sunny beames,
> That in a cloud their light did long time stay,
> Their vapour vaded, shew their golden gleames,
> And through the persant aire shoote forth their
>   azure streames.   (3.9.20)

This drifts toward simple statement, since the event is elaborated with only one simile directly related to the action. The figure here is unlike Ariosto's complex theatrical simile (32. 79-80): Spenser's comparison does not anatomize the revelation's elements, but seeks to create an impression of the event itself—the helmet containing Britomart's hair is like a cloud containing light, the hair like a beam of light suddenly breaking through. Spenser concentrates attention on a visual effect, whereas Ariosto develops specific events narratively and quickly moves to their broadest (or most ludicrous) implications.

Spenser evidently means his figure to imply something very similar to what Ariosto explicitly says: "mostrò la donna aprisse il paradiso." But only four stanzas later does he explicitly mention the "contemplation of diuinitie" (3.9.24). The intervening passage, no less than the initial image of Britomart, illuminates the contrast between Spenser's manner and Ariosto's. Leisure versus brisk dispatch is merely the obvious symptom of their different attitudes toward experience—and especially toward time. Ariosto's brief addition (32.81) to his descriptive similes on Bradamante's hair shows the exact length of its growth since being cut to dress a head wound; suddenly we are reminded of the current episode's temporal setting in Bradamante's story, stretching back to Boiardo's account of her injury (*Orlando innamorato*, 3.5.45-46; 3.8.54-61) through its retelling to Ruggiero in Ariosto's own poem (25.24). The present unfolds with equal lucidity: the master of the castle regulates his behavior according to past knowledge of the heroine, they wait before the fire while food is prepared, and he tells about the customs of the strangely named castle. Spenser, clinging to the implications of his first image of Britomart, all but suspends time as the heroine disarms, is likened to Minerva "late returnd/From slaughter of the Giaunts conquered," and is studied by the court with "hungry vew" (3.9.21-24).[28] Spenser's treatment reveals Britomart's virtue as a visual fact—manifest, outside of time, and above irony—with a universal human response shared by the anonymous court, the audience, and even by Paridell (3.9.25).

Under similar circumstances Milton, in strictly patterned verse, leaps even further than Ariosto into the abstract. It is tempting to think that Milton in his own way is imitating Spenser; if so, it is imitation in its highest form:

> His fair large Front and Eye sublime declar'd
> Absolute rule; and Hyacinthine Locks
> Round from his parted forelock manly hung
> Clust'ring, but not beneath his shoulders broad:
> Shee as a veil down to the slender waist
> Her unadorned golden tresses wore
> Dishevell'd, but in wanton ringlets wav'd
> As the Vine curls her tendrils, which impli'd
> Subjection, but requir'd with gentle sway,
> And by her yielded, by him best receiv'd.
>
> (*P.L.*, 4.300-309)

As Spenser dwells upon appearances and rich surfaces so Milton dwells upon Adam and Eve. But whereas Spenser's concentration is shown in increasingly complex images, Milton's is shown in the syntax. Whatever visual impression the first few lines may generate is concentrated by the significant placement of "clust'ring," a strangely isolated word; but then Milton qualifies, withdraws, and softens the formal closure of his image. The same pattern is repeated with "dishevell'd." Finally, just as he begins to elaborate the visual impression and to repeat this syntactical pattern, Milton shatters the visual surface when he shifts to explanation and abstraction with

---

[28] Spenser's change from *"Bellona"* in the 1590 edition to *"Minerua"* in 1596 would seem to show an effort to avoid any hint of irony in the treatment of Britomart here: Bellona was the goddess's name in her purely bellicose mood. For details see *Variorum*, 3.279 and 425f.

Descriptive or Pictorial?

"which impli'd/Subjection." Even though this word may
have had a more literal, etymological, meaning for Milton
than it does for us, it still seems abstract, and the parallelism
with "clustr'ing" and "dishevell'd" makes it seem more so.
Such abstractness is often present in *Paradise Lost*. In some
ways Milton's poem is easier for the reader than *The Faerie
Queene* simply because Milton is willing to venture into ex-
planation and overt intellectual complication. Spenser relies
on images with an iconography, often confusing or contra-
dictory, that the reader has to puzzle out for himself. Spenser's
explanations are commonly in the form of increased richness
of image.

The stanza on Belphoebe's hair in *The Faerie Queene* is an
example of description which is closer to the pictorial effect
of Focusing than are the passages we have discussed from
Ariosto and Milton—closer too than Spenser's treatment of
Britomart in Malbecco's castle (3.9.20):

> Her yellow lockes crisped, like golden wyre,
> About her shoulders weren loosely shed,
> And when the winde emongst them did inspyre,
> They waued like a penon wide dispred,
> And low behinde her backe were scattered:
> And whether art it were, or heedlesse hap,
> As through the flouring forrest rash she fled,
> In her rude haires sweet flowres themselues did lap,
> And flourishing fresh leaues and blossomes did enwrap.
>
> (2.3.30)

There is a density of description here that we have not encoun-
tered in Ariosto, and Spenser's insistent refusal to depart from
the visual object brings the effect of this stanza close to that
of the one about Acrasia (2.12.77). However, certain differ-
ences prevent this from being a pure example of Focusing:
more important than Belphoebe's apparent motion, is the

59

broken and diffused sequence of images. What at first appears to be a single rich image is compounded by imagining Belphoebe's hair in different states—still, moved, and in motion. The three descriptive units are separated by explanatory clauses, so that we see three separate moments, not one moment perceived in three different ways. Still, each phase of the description contributes to an impression of incrustation; the stanza piles up sensations until finally we not only see the "yellow lockes crisped, like golden wyre," we see them enriched with "flourishing fresh leaues and blossomes." This passage is more descriptive than pictorial even though there are elements of Focusing in it. On a small scale, its imagination of a sight from different spectatorial points of view is similar to one kind of Scanning that I shall discuss later.

I must beg the reader's indulgence to discuss another passage about golden hair in order to refine my definition of Focusing further. It is visually less complex than some pictorial images and perhaps closer to Ariosto or Milton than to Spenser's image of Acrasia's gown; still, the moment early in Book Four when Britomart reveals herself to assembled knights and ladies, belongs in the category of Focused images:

> With that her glistring helmet she vnlaced;
> Which doft, her golden lockes, that were vp bound
> Still in a knot, vnto her heeles downe traced,
> And like a silken veile in compasse round
> About her backe and all her bodie wound:
> Like as the shining skie in summers night,
> What time the dayes with scorching heat abound,
> Is creasted all with lines of firie light,
> That it prodigious seemes in common peoples sight.
>
> (4.1.13)

From the scene at Malbecco's castle (3.9.20) we know that Britomart's suddenly falling hair is a flash of light "like sunny beames," but here the figure is extended until it provides a setting for the revelation as well as a metaphoric correlation between the appearance and its effect on the audience. Suspense operates in the second simile to reinforce the impact of the lightning's sudden "lines of firie light," not only because of the inverted structure in this figure's tiny narrative but because of visual suspense when the background is a uniform "shining skie in summers night." The startling light that emanates from Britomart fixes the attention and for a moment transforms her into a "prodigious" icon, the viewer into a naif. The sequence of images that Spenser groups around Britomart's "golden lockes" when they "vnto her heeles downe traced," is organized almost abstractly enough to prevent precise visualization: from the subject, "golden lockes," to "a silken veile in compasse round" and then to lightning, might seem too discontinuous a sequence. But as he so often does, in this stanza Spenser heightens our visualization of a metaphor by approaching it through others that sustain and redefine it. The first simile shows the exact form of her locks "downe traced," and "shining skie" reasserts their brightness. "Creasted" places the lightning precisely within the second simile yet recalls the visual and psychological experience of Britomart's hair showering about her like a veil from its crest of her helmet.

This enjambment of figures, so characteristic of Spenser's representation of complex visual phenomena, is also observable in an instance of Keats's employment of Focusing from *Lamia*, that narrative poem whose subject has frequently been viewed as the dichotomy between illusion and objective reality. No illusion in *Lamia* is more persuasive than the approach to her Corinthian palace in darkness—the occasion and the subject of the passage, but not an explanation for Keats's pictorial ordering and selection of detail.

> they had arrived before
> A pillar'd porch, with lofty portal door,
> Where hung a silver lamp, whose phosphor glow
> Reflected in the slabbed steps below,
> Mild as a star in water; for so new,
> And so unsullied was the marble hue,
> So through the crystal polish, liquid fine,
> Ran the dark veins, that none but feet divine
> Could e'er have touch'd there. Sounds Aeolian
> Breath'd from the hinges, as the ample span
> Of the wide doors disclos'd a place unknown.[29]

Keats rigorously fixes and limits our attention. Even within the "pillar'd porch, with lofty portal door," we see only a glowing silver lamp with "phosphor glow" and "slabbed steps below." These few articles quickly set forth are the physical occasion for the representation of a fully imagined perceptual enigma. Keats builds this image by comparing present vision with categories established from past experience—at first simple, uncertain, and slightly vague with "mild as a star in water." But then the "unsullied" reflecting "hue" of this marble finally and completely fixes our attention. In this line, too, Keats insinuates that appearances are his subject by the slight archaism of "hue" (meaning not only "color" but "appearance"), an archaism partly confirmed by his use of the word "shew" in an earlier version of the poem.[30] What might be called the "sprung" parallelism of this line to the next calls attention to the suspended syntax and to Keats's uncompleted effort to categorize the "shew" of this reflecting "crystal polish." "Liquid" recalls the original reference to light reflected in water, but the ambiguity of this vision is emphasized by the immediate contrast with "crystal," recalling the

---

[29] *Lamia*, I, 378-388. *The Poetical Works of John Keats*, ed. H. W. Garrod, 2nd ed. (Oxford, 1958).

[30] Garrod, p. 201n.

supposed hardness of the surface. "Liquid," with its connotation of depth and potential movement, is in tension with "polish," which also implies hard thinness of surface in the marble. The sudden introduction of "dark veins" reveals that this pictorial illusion depends upon a minutely limited and intense perception of more extensive objective reality; for these veins appear to be traced "through the crystal polish," but objectively we would think they ran deep into the marble. With a synesthetic imagination more like Shakespeare's than Spenser's, Keats then turns to evoke sensations of touch and hearing reminiscent of those in Enobarbus' description of Cleopatra's barge, but the chief force of his representation is visual. He seems in search of a precise visual impression that is just beyond his grasp. Of course the illusionism is subtle yet pointed in these lines, for illusion is in fact all and the imagined objective reality is false: Lamia's palace has no objective existence.

We may come full circle by looking finally at a passage with an intensive structure almost identical to the Focused image of Acrasia's gown with which we began. In Spenser's revelation of Britomart to Artegall the pictorial effect is particularly noticeable because a complete suspension of action Frames (a term fully defined in the next chapter) a Focused image of Britomart's face surrounded by her brilliant hair:

> And round about the same, her yellow heare
> Hauing through stirring loosd their wonted band,
> Like to a golden border did appeare,
> Framed in goldsmithes forge with cunning hand:
> Yet goldsmithes cunning could not vnderstand
> To frame such subtile wire, so shinie cleare.
> For it did glister like the golden sand,
> The which *Pactolus* with his waters shere,
> Throwes forth vpon the riuage round about him nere.
>
> (4.6.20)

Britomart's "yellow heare" is successively pictured as "a golden border," as "subtile wire, so shinie cleare," and as the golden sand of Pactolus. Alpers has rightly observed that the patent linguistic artificiality of these lines supports the idea that Britomart is a piece of the "goodly workmanship of nature" (4.6.17), and reminds us of conventional Petrarchan praise of female beauty.[31] I would add that Spenser's close observation of a visual phenomenon in this stanza also subverts the simple hyperbole of conventional Petrarchan emblematic conceits. Understatement in the first two lines, particularly the flat descriptiveness of "yellow heare," contrasts with "golden" in the next; the lightly varied doubling of "goldsmithes . . . cunning" in the following two underlines the conventionality of the iconic first simile's distant, unsensitized view of subtle visual experience. The repetition of "goldsmithes cunning" and of "frame," besides the pun on "cunning" and "subtile," points to the inadequacy of the first visualization. This closer view, still with routine diction, reveals fineness of texture and something of its *effect*. The last simile fixes the image and enriches it with a precise view of texture. With the reiterated "golden" Spenser merely underlines our perceptual discovery of the irrelevance of color to the effect that he wants us to observe of brilliant light diffused on or through a lustrous, faceted surface. The poet's refined observation and verbal representation of the liquid appearance of hair struck by bright light is available to the reader if he wonders about the strange emphasis upon the "shere" waters of Pactolus and notices a substructure of references to combined brightness and liquidity in "shere," "cleare," and even in "subtile," which has early associations with liquid and fluid substances.

In the stanza showing Britomart before Artegall, Spenser attempts to represent an indescribable vision by a process of imposing admittedly inadequate figurative schemata upon an

[31] *The Poetry of The Faerie Queene*, pp. 128-130.

imagined sight; the process ends at last with a resort to myth, which allows the poet to say "more golden" in terms whose hyperbole is visually quite specific. Spenser's technique makes it possible for him to lead the imagination far beyond anything that might ordinarily be seen, and to accomplish this not by imitating pictures but by mimesis of the process of visual perception. This poetic method is not and cannot be fundamentally descriptive because Spenser finds partly inadequate those common descriptive terms which, once accepted, become a readily understood shorthand. His imagery is so often pictorial because his shifting metaphorical definitions of visionary experience are closely analogous to our attempts to perceive visual phenomena by categorizing them within a range of familiar schemata. Spenser might well offer us only the last term in many of his linked series of metaphors, but then he would lose the subtle effect of disclosing our distance from Faerie Land while building vivid images of it in our minds. The effect he seeks, somewhat like that of the later artificially youthful portraits of Elizabeth I wearing fantastic satins incrusted with gold, jewels, and embroidery, is to project the imagination a degree beyond the superlatives of the ordinary world (see Frontispiece). Elizabeth wore such dresses not merely to satisfy her marked vanity, but to encourage subjects to see in her the *Idea* of perfect virgin queenship reflecting divine order in secular life.[32] Spenser's invocations to Gloriana embody just such an elevated conception.

> And thou, O fairest Princesse vnder sky,
> In this faire mirrhour maist behold thy face,
> And thine owne realmes in lond of Faery,
> And in this antique Image thy great auncestry.

[32] See Roy C. Strong, *Portraits of Queen Elizabeth I* (Oxford, 1963), especially Plates XVII-XIX. On the history of the term *Idea*, see Erwin Panofsky, *Idea: Ein Beitrag zur Begriffsgeschichte der älteren Kunsttheorie* (Leipzig, 1924), trans. Joseph J. S. Peake (Columbia, S.C., 1968).

Focusing

The which O pardon me thus to enfold
In couert vele, and wrap in shadowes light,
That feeble eyes your glory may behold,
Which else could not endure those beames bright,
But would be dazled with exceeding light.

(2.P.4-5)

The Faerie Queene attempts the delicate task of interpreting
the ideal as heightened, even surreal, human experience. Yet
despite temporary victories, those idealistic aspirations which
imbue the work and emerge forcefully in such a concentrated
allegory as the Garden of Adonis remain generally un-
achieved: a poem so often dark and violent, so marred with
human failure, so preoccupied with the conduct of life, can-
not represent merely abstract Christian or Platonic ideals.
Elements of the marvelous in Spenser's story should not dis-
tract us from his remarkable incarnation of the particulars
of life in a chivalric setting; nor should we forget that the
invocation of Arthurian ideals and the appearance of imagery
from medieval pageantry in ceremonial life at Elizabeth's
court would have narrowed the gulf between ordinary experi-
ence and Spenser's fiction for many of his first readers.[33]
Spenser indicates in the various exordia that *The Faerie
Queene* is a work of exploration and discovery, and he uses
pictorial imagery much as he uses medieval settings and
chivalric ideals to fix our aspiring relationship to Faerie. His
own sense of discovery, perhaps most apparent in his images
of the rising sun, is one of the poem's engaging features—
quite different from Ariosto's pervasive control of his well-
mapped action. Spenser, as Robert M. Durling says in another
context, "never assumes the position of absolute dominion in
the world of the poem, which provides so much interest in

[33] See Rosemond Tuve, *Allegorical Imagery* (Princeton, 1966), pp.
340-342, 388-389, and citations, on Spenser and Elizabethan chivalry.

the *Orlando furioso*."[34] Spenser attempts to build in the reader's imagination the experience of ideal human action in a visionary setting; he does not aspire simply to Platonic abstractions. The Proem to Book Two asserts his role as mediator between ordinary experience and the golden world he leads us to discover, and as a caution to skeptical readers compares Faerie Land with New Worlds which "were, when no man did them know":

> Of Faerie lond yet if he more inquire,
> By certaine signes here set in sundry place
> He may it find; ne let him then admire,
> But yield his sence to be too blunt and bace,
> That n'ote without an hound fine footing trace.
>
> (2.P.4)

Spenser is by no means mystical. His allegory is secular, and though it may at times reflect the ideal order of a Platonic universe, it is founded in careful observation of human action in the phenomenal world.

[34] *The Figure of the Poet in Renaissance Epic* (Cambridge, Mass., 1965), p. 216.

CHAPTER THREE

The Visual Field: Framing

James J. Gibson speaks of the familiar, relatively stable continuum which he calls the "visual world" as a dialectical fusion of objective visibilia with our innate and learned capacities for visual discrimination. He contrasts the visual world with the bounded "visual field," which is an introspective and transitory mode of seeing. The visual field "is simply the pictorial mode of visual perception, and it depends in the last analysis not on conditions of stimulation but on conditions of attitude. The visual field is the product of the chronic habit of civilized men of seeing the world as a picture." The visual field is singular, fixed in time, bounded by margins, and governed by perspective: "so far from being the basis, it is a kind of *alternative* to ordinary perception."[1] The purpose of this chapter is to discuss some literary manifestations of the "chronic habit" that Gibson mentions, and especially to show how literary images can be given fixed boundaries. Such images are Framed because they command a different kind of attention than do their surroundings, not because they are set in an ornamental border. Even in the case of actual pictures, the frame of wood or gold is merely a formal recognition of the picture's discrete ontology. These literary images, like the visual field, are fixed within boundaries and therefore

---

[1] "The Visual Field and the Visual World," *Psychological Review*, LIX (1952), 149-151. Quoted by E. H. Gombrich, *Art and Illusion*, 2nd ed. (Princeton, 1961), p. 328. See also Gibson, "Pictures, Perspective, and Perception," *Daedalus*, LXXXIX (1960) 216-227; and, for the basic distinction between the bounded field of the fixed eye and our construction of the visual world from a combination of fields see, *The Perception of the Visual World* (Boston, 1950), pp. 26-43.

have a special perceptual status—a quality shared in some degree by Focused imagery for the simple reason that no poetic imitation of "ordinary perception" could be perfectly continuous and unbounded.

Framed images suspend our attention within the narrow visual range of a formally coherent spatial configuration or some other formally closed encounter with the perceptual world. Breaks in narrative set them apart—most strikingly at moments of reversal in the action. Framed images are similar in nature to emblems, conceived either as enigmatic pictures or as rhetorical figures, but they meet additional defining requirements. They are more than iconographic signs or emblematic conceits, although they may include such devices. These basic restrictions should prevent our definition from expanding too flexibly; one reason that I have chosen the term "Framed" rather than "Emblematic" is that the familiar terminology is often used so loosely.

Were it characterized in one distilled phrase, Framing might be called the creation of a formally or spatially coherent image at a juncture of marked interruption or reversal of action. In form it is corollary to that incrustation of images at moments of narrative suspension which I have called Focusing. Spenser sometimes combines the two techniques, even though the stasis of Framing at first does not seem compatible with the involution, the careful avoidance of methodical listing and diagrammatic formulas, characteristic of Focusing. Both kinds of images flourish in the atmosphere of demarcated literary space which Angus Fletcher shows to be typical of allegory because of its tendency to employ arbitrarily closed forms; he concludes from an analysis based upon psychological models that *The Divine Comedy* and *The Faerie Queene* show this characteristic most strikingly, "because not only do they exhibit it along the way, by what I would call a 'segregation of parts' (e.g., the stanza forms of both poems), but they both are intended to close with a final homecoming in an ideal world." Fletcher has also associated allegorical writing with the psychoanalytic analogue of compulsion or fixation, the defining symptom of which is highly orderly, almost ritualistic behavior.[2] At a more detailed level, William Empson is not alone in observing the exclusive "fixity" of the form, and it is commonplace to note the Spenserian stanza's firmly stopped ending.[3] As A. C. Hamilton says, the mosaic structure of Spenser's self-centered stanzas and their tightly interlocking, self-contained rhymes, "make the stanza *stand*, fixed for the moment as a globe for our contemplation, or as a painting to be read in spatial terms. It is not a point within a narrative line, begotten by the last stanza and begetting the next."[4] Spenser's nearly compulsive anatomizing of visual experience may be seen to spring from the psychological roots indicated by Fletcher and to be embodied in the peculiar form of his stanza.

The Nature of Framing

Perhaps the best way to sketch the chief rhetorical features of Framed imagery is to contrast the passage in *The Faerie Queene* where Britomart is revealed to Artegall with Tasso's treatment of similar materials in *Gerusalemme liberata*.

The wicket stroke vpon her helmet chaunst,
And with the force, which in it selfe it bore,
Her ventayle shard away, and thence forth glaunst
A downe in vaine, ne harm'd her any more.

[2] *Allegory: The Theory of a Symbolic Mode* (Ithaca, 1964), p. 176 and pp. 279-303.
[3] *Seven Types of Ambiguity*, 2nd ed. (London, 1947), pp. 33-34.
[4] *The Structure of Allegory in the Faerie Queene* (Oxford, 1961), p. 14.

With that her angels face, vnseene afore,
Like to the ruddie morne appeard in sight,
Deawed with siluer drops, through sweating sore,
But somewhat redder, then beseem'd aright,
Through toylesome heate and labour of her weary fight.

And round about the same, her yellow heare
Hauing through stirring loosd their wonted band,
Like to a golden border did appeare,
Framed in goldsmithes forge with cunning hand:
Yet goldsmithes cunning could not vnderstand
To frame such subtile wire, so shinie cleare.
For it did glister like the golden sand,
The which *Pactolus* with his waters shere,
Throwes forth vpon the riuage round about him nere.

And as his hand he vp againe did reare,
Thinking to worke on her his vtmost wracke,
His powrelesse arme benumbd with secret feare
From his reuengefull purpose shronke abacke,
And cruell sword out of his fingers slacke
Fell downe to ground, as if the steele had sence,
And felt some ruth, or sence his hand did lacke,
Or both of them did thinke, obedience
To doe to so diuine a beauties excellence.

(4.6.19-21)

After the fourth line there is jarring suspension of the action, which does not resume for fourteen lines. Before Spenser is able to proceed he seems compelled to present an isolated image of revelation, a visible cause for the peripeteia to follow. The effect is doubly striking because nine of the enclosed lines present a Focused image which is conceived as the fixed center of a bounded or Framed visual field. However, our attention is first arrested by controverted expectation and interrupted narrative progression: we expect action and we get suspension—a kind of poetic gasp of amazement. Spenser suspends our attention in a narrow visual range by excluding us from the minds of his characters and forcing us into an experience correlative to Artegall's. The meaning of the episode at first seems distilled into the Framed image of Britomart's face, yet, as I observed in the previous chapter, the language and imagery of this passage subvert the conventional hyperbole of its Petrarchan iconography. When the action continues in stanza twenty-one, the narrator seems to turn to the psychological import of the scene; but then he offers only speculation, as if even he does not have immediate access to the characters' minds and must rely on appearances which contain meanings never fully revealed. As we try to get a view of this strange Faerie world, it seems possible that any of the proposed alternatives may be the correct interpretation of Artegall's inaction, possible that "the steele had sence . . . or sence his hand did lacke," and also that "both of them did thinke, obedience/ To doe." Only in the next stanza do we see that this last is correct and conclusive.

Reference to the Renaissance concept of *imago Dei* best explicates this passage: it reveals a human image through which the goodness of God shines, an appearance symbolically identical with the reality behind it. Britomart becomes such a religious image for Artegall, who "At last fell humbly downe vpon his knee,/ And of his wonder made religion" (4.6.22). According to Thomas P. Roche, Jr. the effect upon Artegall "is that of a religious conversion or revelation, and . . . Spenser intends us to see that the inception of love is such a revelation, dazzling and illuminating, relating the beings involved to a more primary Love that we may merely signify through images of light."[5] If this interpretation is correct, Spenser's

[5] *The Kindly Flame* (Princeton, 1964), p. 94 and pp. 88-95. Roche cites Arnold Williams, *The Common Expositor* (Chapel Hill, 1948), to support his interpretation.

pictorialism in the scene is far more than ornamental. As he returns us to the sensuous and experiential bases of a conventionalized image, he asserts its intrinsic value and comments upon the inadequacy of unexamined conventionality. Human love is an aspect of divine love, human beauty an aspect of divine beauty, and the "inception of love" is analogous to religious conversion; but Artegall's merely conventional response to his stunning experience is based upon literal acceptance of a metaphor the figurative force and sensuous origin of which Spenser revives for the reader. This sophisticated rhetorical arrangement of visual image and action forces the reader to participate in that psychological suspension characteristic of romantic and religious discovery. Framing makes verse-time as inessential to the total poetic experience as clocktime is to experiences of actual discovery, when time may seem infinitely compressed or extended. Verisimilitude undoubtedly imposes limits on such effects, but Spenser is well within them here. The creation of a golden image of Britomart at the moment of her revelation to Artegall is especially appropriate: Artegall kneels before a dazzling and divine image of Love which is represented in the poetic medium as a picture set off from and interrupting the action.

Interpretation of Spenserian images depends chiefly upon the linguistic and narrative context. In stanza nineteen we are told of Britomart's "angels face," and careful reading shows that the presentation is unconventional, but not until Artegall kneels can we build a coherent interpretation:

> And he himselfe long gazing thereupon,
> At last fell humbly downe vpon his knee,
> And of his wonder made religion,
> Weening some heauenly goddesse he did see,
> Or else vnweeting, what it else might bee.
>
> (4.6.22)

Framing

Artegall's action Frames the image and also sets it in an unbounded field of experience or, as it were, objectifies it; before, despite close reading and a knowledge of Britomart's identity, the reader inclines to follow Artegall in "Weening some heauenly goddesse he did see." The surface is phenomenally complex, and there is no omniscient interpreter to help us penetrate it. The narrator's point of view is at times absorbed into Artegall's; at other times it seems to be separate. The narrator is a sensitive interpreter of surfaces, but, as in stanza twenty-one, he often leaves us uncertain of the ultimate significance of what he observes.

Like so many Spenserian images, this one of Britomart has no self-evident meaning. Its superficial iconography is merely an element in the paradoxical synthesis that we call the poet's meaning. Even learned readers might find purely iconographic interpretation of this isolated image difficult: though we can guess at implications, the validity of any single explanation would be difficult to demonstrate. Because of the diversity of Renaissance symbolic systems as well as Spenser's ambivalence toward traditional iconography, his allegory cannot count on instant and fixed symbolic recognition from the reader. This particular stanza reveals much more about the immediate sensuous impact of a marvelous appearance of something golden than it does about the iconographic significance of that appearance. The informed reader of Chaucer's iconic description of Alceste would have less difficulty; a knowledge of the context would lead to subtler discriminations and to elegant additions, but the basic significance of the image and its primary role in the meaning of the work is clear. Spenser, despite the medieval atmosphere he successfully evokes, so firmly asserts the equality as forms of knowledge of sensation and idea—experience and abstraction—that his allegory can only be understood as a product of Renaissance culture.

It is interesting to compare this confrontation between Britomart and Artegall with the recognition scene in *Gerusalemme*

74

liberata where Tancred mortally wounds Clorinda, and realizes what he has done only as he lifts her visor to offer water fetched in his helmet from a nearby brook:

> Egli v'accorse e l'elmo empié nel fonte,
> e tornò mesto al grande ufficio e pio.
> Tremar sentì la man, mentre la fronte
> non conosciuta ancor sciolse e scoprio.
> La vide, la conobbe, e restò senza
> e voce e moto. Ahi vista! ahi conoscenza!
>
> Non morì già, ché sue virtuti accolse
> tutte in quel punto e in guardia al cor le mise,
> a premendo il suo affanno a dar si volse
> vita con l'acqua a chi co 'l ferro uccise.
> Mentre egli il suon de' sacri detti sciolse,
> colei di gioia trasmutossi, e rise;
> e in atto di morir lieto e vivace,
> dir parea: "S'apre il cielo: io vado in pace."
>
> D'un bel pallore ha il bianco volto asperso,
> come a' gigli sarian miste viole,
> e gli occhi al cielo affisa, e in lei converso
> sembra per la pietate il cielo e 'l sole;
> e la man nuda e fredda alzando verso
> il cavaliero in vece di parole
> gli dà pegno di pace. . . .[6]

> Thither he ran and filled his helmet wide,
> And quick return'd to do that work of grace:
> With trembling hands her beaver he untied,
> Which done, he saw, and seeing knew her face,
> And lost therewith his speech and moving quite;
> O woeful knowledge! ah unhappy sight!

---

[6] Torquato Tasso, *Opere*, III, ed. Bruno Maier (Milan: Rizzoli Editore, 1963), 12.67-69; trans. Edward Fairfax (Carbondale, Ill., 1962). All references are to these editions.

He died not, but all his strength unites,
And to his virtues gave his heart in guard;
Bridling his grief, with water he requites
The life that he bereft with iron hard:
And while the sacred words the knight recites,
The nymph to heav'n with joy herself prepar'd;
And as her life decays her joys increase;
She smil'd and said—Farewell! I die in peace.

As violets blue 'mongst lilies pure men throw,
So paleness 'midst her native white begun.
Her looks to heav'n she cast; their eyes, I trow,
Downward for pity bent both heav'n and sun.
Her naked hand she gave the knight, in show
Of love and peace. . . .

Tasso might well have suspended a description or an image in the central stanza, and with good effect; however, he does not organize material as Spenser does. He is fascinated with the dynamics of action and psychology in narrative, so we see Clorinda not set off and depicted as a visual wonder, but in a developing personal relationship with Tancred. In Tasso's scene there is an exclamation of amazement, but no suspension of action and no Framed image. Indeed, it seems to be a mark of Tancred's strength of character that he does the proper service without delay. The lines "D'un bel pallore ha il bianco volto asperso,/ come a'gigli sarian miste viole," are descriptive, but in context even this figure of Icon is part of the narrative of Clorinda's approaching death. Tasso's narrator ranges so freely through the minds of his characters that it is difficult even to tell whether he or Tancred speaks the words "Ahi vista! ahi conoscenza!" Of course we are told that Tancred has lost his voice, but at this point the narrator seems almost absorbed into his character. The detachment and concern for visible surfaces so notable in Spenser are absent

in Tasso; the two poets use similar materials in entirely differ-
ent ways.

An earlier encounter between Tancred and Clorinda per-
haps parallels more closely the encounter between Britomart
and Artegall, and will help us further define Framing as a
device of Spenserian pictorialism. The encounter takes place
when Tancred and Clorinda collide in battle:

> Ferirsi a le visiere, e i tronchi in alto
> volaro e parte nuda ella ne resta:
> ché, rotti i lacci a l'elmo suo, d'un salto
> (mirabil colpo!) ei le balzò di testa;
> e le chiome dorate al vento sparse,
> giovane donna in mezzo 'l campo apparse.

> Lampeggiar gli occhi e folgorar gli sguardi,
> dolci ne l'ira; or che sarian nel riso?
> Tancredi, a che pur pensi? a che pur guardi?
> non riconosci tu l'altero viso?
> Quest'è pur quel bel volto onde tutt'ardi:
> tuo core il dica, ov'è il suo essempio inciso.
> Questa è colei che rinfrescar la fronte
> vedesti già nel solitario fonte.

> Ei ch'al cimiero ed al dipinto scudo
> non badò prima, or lei veggendo impetra;
> ella quanto può meglio il capo ignudo
> si ricopre, e l'assale; ed ei s'arretra.
> Va contra gli altri, e rota il ferro crudo;
> ma però da lei pace non impetra,
> che minacciosa il segue, e: "Volgi" grida;
> e di due morti in un punto lo sfida.

> Percosso, il cavalier non ripercote,
> né sì dal ferro a riguardarsi attende,
> come a guardar i begli occhi e le gote
> ond'Amor l'arco inevitabil tende.   (3.21-24)

Framing

Upon their helms they crack'd their lances long,
And from her head her guilden casque he kest,
For every lace he broke and every thong,
And in the dust threw down her plumed crest,
About her shoulders shone her golden locks,
Like sunny beams on alabaster rocks.

Her looks with fire, her eyes with lightning blaze,
Sweet was her wrath, what then would be her smile?
Tancred, whereon think'st thou? what dost thou gaze?
Hast thou forget her in so short a while?
The same is she, the shape of whose sweet face
The god of love did in thy heart compile:
The same that left thee by the cooling stream,
Safe from sun's heat, but scorch'd with beauty's beam.

The prince well knew her, though her painted shield
And golden helm he had not mark'd before;
She sav'd her head, and with her axe, well steel'd,
Assail'd the knight: but her the knight forbore;
'Gainst other foes he prov'd him through the field,
Yet she for that refrained ne'er the more,
But following, Turn thee, cried, in ireful wise;
And so at once she threats to kill him twice.

Not once the baron lift his armed hand
To strike the maid, but gazing on her eyes,
Where lordly Cupid seem'd in arms to stand,
No way to ward or shun her blows he tries.

Tasso certainly does not transform Clorinda into a religious image. Still, the action seems to be suspended much as Spenser's is, and one stanza is definitely set off from its neighbors. But the stanza could hardly be called pictorial—or even descriptive. In part, this has to do with Tasso's relative lack of emphasis on complex visual phenomena. Only two lines are devoted to actual description, and in the rest of the stanza the narrator addresses Tancred to remind him—and, more importantly, us—of Clorinda's identity. The narrator psychologizes Tancred's amazement and seems to echo what the cavalier might be thinking in the instant preceding complete recognition. It is possible to interpret the line, "Tancredi, a che pur pensi? a che pur guardi?" as implying that Tancred stops for a moment and stares idly. If this is correct, there is no break in the action but rather a point of emphasis in the narrative. Visual details, such as "Lampeggiar gli occhi e folgorar gli sguardi," serve chiefly as associative links to previous important psychological moments: e.g., when Clorinda's gaze first struck Tancred. As in the death scene visual detail is diffused, integrated with the action, and employed in the poet's representation of character, not concentrated into Framed or Focused units. Images and similes serve Tasso as rhetorical links (3.21) or even as moments in the action of the poem (12.69). Compounded visual images in Spenser are a medium of discovery and can have enthymemic force; they are likely to carry more sensuous effect and more of the narrative's ultimate significance than in Tasso. It is partly because the relation of surfaces and appearances to what they hide or reveal is so important to Spenser that suspension of action becomes the basis of a pictorial device.

The pictorial effect of Framing depends upon the exact nature of the suspension of action and upon what fills the resulting poetic space. Let us summarize by returning briefly to Artegall's recognition scene. It is essential in Framing that the main action be interrupted completely and that the interval contain a formally coherent visual experience. The apparent break in the scene from Tasso contains various elements—even part of the main action—but when Britomart is revealed to Artegall, there is no suggestion of action between "ne harm'd her any more" and "And as his hand he vp againe did reare." The intervening experience may be Artegall's alone; more likely it is the narrator's interpretation of what everyone's experience would or should be at such a moment. This representation of visual experience is not gratuitous, but in itself is the reason for suspending the action and the point at which the action turns in a new direction: the image of Britomart is the reason that "His powrelesse arme benumbd with secret feare/ From his reuengefull purpose shronke abacke." Pictures in Spenser's poetic world are reasons, not ornaments. If we skipped from "ne harm'd her any more" to "And as his hand he vp againe did reare," we might safely assume that surprise accounts for much of what ensues, but it would be difficult to account for "At last fell humbly downe vpon his knee,/ And of his wonder made religion" (4.6.22). Rosemond Tuve has written that "seriousness about the philosophical and metaphysical purport of the images in the *Faerie Queene*" is one of its distinguishing features.[7] I would be even more emphatic. It is typical of Spenser's procedure in *The Faerie Queene* to depend for crucial responses, from the questing knights and from the reader, upon partly or wholly unexplained visual images. In such a poetic climate any interruption at a pivotal moment can prove the occasion for Framing a formally coherent image which illuminates the following action.

Emblems in Poetry

Some readers will by now have asked what the relationship between Framed images and so called "emblematic images" may be. The answer requires an excursus beginning appropriately in Renaissance style with the first meanings of a word; "emblem" is from the Greek and, to quote Geoffrey Whitney's definition of 1586, "is as muche to saye in Englishe as *To set in, or to put in*: properlie ment by suche figures, or workes, as are wroughte in plate, or in stones in the pauementes, or on the

[7] *Allegorical Imagery* (Princeton, 1966), pp. 48-49.

waules, or suche like, for the adorning of the place: hauinge
some wittie deuise expressed with cunning woorkemanship,
somethinge obscure to be perceiued at first, whereby, when
with further consideration it is vnderstood, it maie the greater
delighte the beholuder."[8] Although theorists did use the word
loosely to mean a picture combined with a complementary
poem, their usage ordinarily referred to a picture with a covert
significance. In emblem books the picture was often glossed
with a motto or poem.[9]

Both the verbal and visual elements in an emblem book
function as different classes of "words," but modern viewers
tend to accept whatever formal and sensuous values the artist
has bestowed upon the emblem and to ignore its demand to
function as conceptual, quasi-verbal discourse.[10] Although

---

[8] *A Choice of Emblemes* (Leyden, 1586), sig. **4 recto.

[9] Rosemary Freeman, *English Emblem Books* (London, 1948), pp. 37-
38, says "In seventeenth century terminology it was generally the picture
alone that was the 'Emblem', the motto was called the 'Word', and the
poet added Verses or 'moralised the emblem'." Terms varied in practice,
but the principle remained the same: the "emblem"—as we would call
the combined figure, motto, and poem—had a minimum of two parts,
the "Emblem" and the "Word." Other terms were "Figure" (*Figura*)
and "Motto" (*Lemma* or *Vox*). The basic theory of emblem writing
was stated by Alciati in *De Verborum Significatione* (1530): "Words
symbolize, and things are symbolized by them. But things can also
be symbolized by other things, as exemplified by the hieroglyphics of
Horum and Chaeremon. To demonstrate this, we have compiled a book
entitled *Emblemata*." Translation by Mario Praz, *Encyclopedia of
World Art*, iv, 727; the Latin appears in his *Studies in Seventeenth-
Century Imagery*, 2nd ed. (Rome, 1964), p. 22.

[10] In *The Life and Art of Albrecht Dürer* (Princeton, 1955), p. 173,
Erwin Panofsky describes how the figurative parts of emblems func-
tion as signs in the visual arts, as "images which refuse to be accepted
as representations of mere things but demand to be interpreted as
vehicles of concepts; they are tolerated by most modern critics, as a
rule, only if incorporated in a work so rich in 'atmosphere' that it can,
after all, be 'enjoyed' without a detailed explanation." In another essay
Panofsky gives a more elaborate definition: he says that the emblem
"partakes of the nature of the symbol (only that it is particular rather

pictorial vividness and aesthetic sophistication enhance the
effectiveness of an emblem, they are not essential to its nature,
as the artistic crudeness of many successful emblem books
shows. Thus, the naming or describing of symbolic objects
or scenes with no attempt at formal coherence, at innovative
presentation of traditional forms, or at the imitation of phe-
nomenal surfaces, may move us to call a work of literature
emblematic. However, pictorialism as it is defined in this study
exists only when the poet thrusts the specifically visual impact
of his materials upon us.[11] That the necessary components
of emblems are descriptive as opposed to pictorial is manifest
in Giordano Bruno's *De gli eroici furori*, a series of dialogues
arranged in sections which closely correspond to the parts of
an elaborate emblem book: an emblem is described verbally
and its motto is given; the emblem is developed in the con-
ceits of a Petrarchan poem, and the meaning of both emblem
and poem is explained in a commentary. Frances A. Yates has
suggested some of the important implications which this book,
published in London in 1585 and dedicated to Sir Philip Sid-
ney, may have for our understanding of Elizabethan sonnet
sequences; her discussion of the work conveys a strong im-

than universal), the puzzle (only that it is not quite so difficult), the
apophthegm (only that it is visual rather than verbal), and the proverb
(only that it is erudite rather than commonplace)." *Meaning in the
Visual Arts* (Garden City, N.Y., 1955), p. 148. This definition is based
upon Alciati's commentator Claudius Minos; see Andrea Alciati, *Em-
blemata . . . cvm Commentariis . . . per Clavdivm Minoem* (Antwerp,
1577), p. 42.

[11] Symbolic imagery fascinated serious thinkers in the Renaissance,
and inspired a large body of theoretical writing which includes many
books on emblems, *imprese*, and hieroglyphics. My generalizations
about emblems are not intended as a summary of Renaissance theory.
On this subject see Robert J. Clements, *Picta Poesis: Literary and
Humanistic Theory in Renaissance Emblem Books* (Rome, 1960). On
the special status of visual images in the period see E. H. Gombrich,
"Icones Symbolicae: The Visual Image in Neo-Platonic Thought,"
JWCI, xi (1948), 163-192.

pression of the emblematically charged atmosphere of the period.[12] Emblem books are only one manifestation of that atmosphere. In view of their heavy dependence upon and close relation to the *Greek Anthology*, Petrarchan conceits,[13] and other literary sources—in addition to the possibility of their being produced by entirely literary means—it seems mistaken to emphasize the formal, pictorial elements of emblems as opposed to the iconographic in tracing the origins of Spenserian pictorialism. As one critic has said, "the very grotesqueness of many of the emblems is testimony to the fact that the conceit preceded—and was therefore independent of—its graphic expression."[14] We first notice Renaissance emblem

[12] "The Emblematic Conceit in Giordano Bruno's *De Gli Eroici Furori* and in the Elizabethan Sonnet Sequences," *JWCI*, vi (1943), 101-121. The work may be found in Giordano Bruno, *Opere italiane*, ed. G. Gentile (Bari, 1908), ii, 288-488. It has been translated by L. Williams, *The Heroic Enthusiasts*, 2 vols. (London, 1887-1889). I have not been able to see this translation.

[13] See Yates, pp. 105-108, and *Studies in Seventeenth-Century Imagery*, pp. 13-14, on the importance of Petrarchan conceits as a source for emblems.

[14] Joseph A. Mazzeo, "A Critique of Some Modern Theories of Metaphysical Poetry," in *Seventeenth Century English Poetry*, ed. William R. Keast (New York, 1962), p. 71. The purpose of my discussion is not to denigrate emblem books, but to establish that despite their visual referents and their use of the media of the visual arts they are literary in nature. A great emblem may attract our attention and increase our interest in its meaning by a resonant combination of traditional iconographic materials and emotional complexity, but the greatest of emblems shares its fundamentally literary character with the crudest. However, the purely formal aesthetic appeal of surface can reduce the importance of a work's emblematic character to a secondary level for most viewers, no matter how fascinating that character may be. For example, we attend to Titian's *Allegory of Prudence* (National Gallery, London) primarily for its magnificent execution of an elaborate threefold self-portrait. Of course, the emblematic level remains important, and Titian's *Prudence* has a personal as well as a general moral significance; as Panofsky says at the end of his essay on the picture, only patient study reveals to us "the beauty and appropriateness of its diction." Panofsky goes on to speak directly

books because of their pictures, but the purely poetic emblem productions of the age derived from the ancient tradition of ecphrastic poetry must also have been important factors in the keen figural awareness of the sixteenth century. Yates's discovery of the probable emblematic interpretation of Petrarchan conceits in Elizabethan poetry should make us aware that we are passing over many figures which may once have called emblems to the mind's eye.[15]

The relationship of emblems to the pictorial technique that I call Framing can perhaps be clarified by reference to a description of rhetorical terms by John Hoskins (1566-1638). According to Hoskins' commonplace definition, Allegory, Metaphor, and Emblem[16] are similar rhetorical figures; he says that "ALLEGORY is the continual following of a metaphor . . . through the sentence, or through many sentences." His example is roughly based on Sidney: "Philoclea was so environed with sweet rivers of virtue as that she could neither be battered nor undermined." Further, the literary figure

---

to my purpose when he says that "in a work of art . . . the distribution of color and lines, light and shade, volumes and planes, however delightful as a visual spectacle must also be understood as carrying a more-than-visual meaning." The very choice of the word "diction" indicates that the "more-than-visual meaning," like the motto or "soul" of the emblem, is thought of as literary. See "Titian's *Allegory of Prudence*: A Postscript," p. 168, in *Meaning in the Visual Arts*, pp. 146-168, for a brilliant exposition of the painting.

[15] Yates, "The Emblematic Conceit," p. 103, says that "a large number of the conventional sonnet images are used by Bruno . . . as emblems of mystical experience. Yet if the poetry of the *Eroici furori* were to be printed by itself, without the prose emblems and the explanatory prose commentaries, we should have what would appear to be a kind of sonnet sequence (although not all the verses are in sonnet form), very obscure and difficult to follow, yet highly conventional in the conceits and images which it uses."

[16] I mean the capitalized word to indicate the rhetorical figure strictly defined and the uncapitalized word to indicate a representation in a medium of the visual arts or in literature.

"Emblem" is, in effect, a separation of the parts of Allegory's continued metaphor into isolated units: "An emblem, an allegory, a similitude, a fable, and a poet's tale differ thus: an EMBLEM is but the one part of the similitude, the other part (viz., the application) expressed indifferently and jointly in one sentence, with words some proper to the one part, some to the other. . . . In the former example, plant a castle compassed with rivers and let the word be, *Nec obsidione nec cuniculis* (neither by siege nor undermining): that is an emblem, the proper terms of the one part. Lay it as it is in Sir Philip S[idney]: *Philoclea's virtue*, the proper terms of the one part; *environed, rivers, battered, undermined*, the terms of the other part; all these terms in one sentence and it is an allegory."[17] A Framed image, separated from surrounding poetic terrain by suspension or interruption, serving as the focal point of the action, and requiring explanation to clarify its meaning seems close to the figure Hoskins calls "Emblem." Framing is similar, though Hoskins seems to think of his figure on a very small scale. The difference is that, whatever their scale, emblematic images are typically descriptive groupings of iconographic signs. They are not by nature formally or spatially coherent, although, as we shall see, Spenser sometimes makes them into Framed or Focused images. My term "Framing" is directly descended from Hoskins' "Emblem," but it is more specific.

Modern critics have been inclined to talk about allegory in

[17] *Directions for Speech and Style*, ed. Hoyt H. Hudson (Princeton, 1935), pp. 9-10. Freeman identifies Hoskins' rhetorical bias as an emblem theorist: "From the very beginning it had been uncertain whether the form derived from Egyptian hieroglyphics or from the Greek anthology, whether, that is, its pictorial or its rhetorical side was of prime importance. This doubt resulted in a dual classification: emblems were associated by some critics, notably Abraham Fraunce, with insignia, arms, symbols and hieroglyphics, and by others, for instance by John Hoskins . . . with allegories, similitudes, fables and poets' tales." *English Emblem Books*, pp. 85-86.

the broadest possible terms, and to absorb figures like Emblem as part of Allegory without describing their specific characteristics. For instance, Angus Fletcher's chief concern in his brief discussion of emblems is to show how the emblematic slides into and is absorbed by the allegorical: "Unless he is a pure emblematist, the poet is likely to complicate his poem, so that the just weighing of merits becomes a process with several moments. . . . The poet makes what Spenser called 'a pleasing analysis of all,' and in the course of this analysis an action unfolds, with agents to carry it."[18] In other words, a metaphor extended in time becomes an Allegory.[19] Fletcher's statement at first seems satisfactory, but it glosses over a distinction that Hoskins has not missed in his words on similitudes. An emblem remains an emblem whether it underwritten by allegorical verse, an explanation embedded in a long poem, a motto, a name, or even nothing. Hoskins was voicing the general understanding that in emblem books, as well as in other literature, the picture or the verbal figure alone was the emblem, while the motto or accompanying poem was the "Word." Emblems could be iconic verbal images, but usually they were pictures that presented a momentary interpretive challenge in order to make a moral point forcefully: *"Emblems* are generall conceiptes rather of moral matters then perticulare deliberations: rather to giue credit to the wit, then to reueale the secretes of the minde."[20] The moral point of the emblem is

[18] *Allegory*, p. 26. In Edwin Honig's *Dark Conceit* (Evanston, 1959), a similarly inclusive approach entails reference to the allegorical character of emblems, but no discussion of Emblem as a figure; see especially pp. 71-72 and 100.

[19] Although Fletcher attacks this notion in another chapter, at this moment he seems to follow it. He later challenges the old rhetorical tradition, represented by Hoskins, which classified allegory as an extended metaphor or a sequence of closely related metaphors. See *Allegory*, Chapter Two, "The Cosmic Image."

[20] Paolo Giovio, *The Worthy Tract of Paulus Iovius* . . . , trans. Samuel Daniel (London, 1585), Preface by N. W., sig. *vi verso.

almost always driven home by a poem, or at the least a motto, but picture and explanation are formally separate. Confusion about "emblematic" poetry arises because the figure and the motto are presented verbally, in the same medium.

In *The Merchant of Venice* a miniature of Portia appears which hovers on the boundary between emblematic description and Framing. The image serves as a literal *emblem* in the action of the play when Bassanio finds it in the leaden casket with an accompanying scroll containing the "Word":

> Fair Portia's counterfeit! What demi-god
> Hath come so near creation? move these eyes?
> Or whether (riding on the balls of mine)
> Seem they in motion? Here are sever'd lips
> Parted with sugar breath,—so sweet a bar
> Should sunder such sweet friends: here in her hairs
> The painter plays the spider, and hath woven
> A golden mesh t'entrap the hearts of men
> Faster than gnats in cobwebs,—but her eyes!
> How could he see to do them? having made one,
> Methinks it should have power to steal both his
> And leave itself unfurnish'd: yet look how far
> The substance of my praise doth wrong this shadow
> In underprizing it, so far this shadow
> Doth limp behind the substance. Here's the scroll,
> The continent and summary of my fortune.[21]

The portrait's appearance marks a turning point in the action of the play, and the opening of the casket, with everyone held in suspense, creates a kind of Frame. The recurring references to Portia's eyes give the descriptive elements a certain formal coherence, but the comparison to an actual character on the stage distracts us from the verbal image. However, in dra-

[21] *The Arden Edition*, ed. John Russell Brown (London, 1955), III.ii.115-130.

matic context the emblem's function is not simply to point to a beauty we can already witness, but to impose Bassanio's vision of Portia upon us. Although this emblem is suspended between the pictorial and the descriptive, the context is contrived to make it seem pictorial. In general, Shakespeare's pictorial techniques define single visual experiences less sharply than do Spenser's, and Shakespeare more often appeals to senses other than sight to enhance his effects. In this respect, Enobarbus' description of Cleopatra is an excellent example of his method.

When Scudamour in *The Faerie Queene* describes his approach to the Temple of Venus and the plain before it, an image with inscription is presented, like Shakespeare's emblem of Portia, as a feature of the poem's plot:

> Before that Castle was an open plaine,
> And in the midst thereof a piller placed;
> On which this shield, of many sought in vaine,
> The shield of Loue, whose guerdon me hath graced,
> Was hangd on high with golden ribbands laced;
> And in the marble stone was written this,
> With golden letters goodly well enchaced,
> *Blessed the man that well can vse his blis*:
> *Whose euer be the shield, faire Amoret be his.*
>
> (4.10.8)

The narrative context prevents this emblematic stanza from being a true example of Framing. It is part of Scudamour's narration of his adventure, and the events and experiences he relates are formed as recollections, not shown as perceptions in order of occurrence. Thus, Scudamour first describes the Temple of Venus, then its defenses, and finally the plain in front of the castle. The emblem he sees inspires him to action and is neatly linked to the following events, but it is part of a descriptive sequence which is logically ordered as recollection and which inspires him to a quest the substance of which he already knows. The things described in the stanza do not change the circumstances of Scudamour's quest, since he knows what he seeks and shortly finds it. There is no sudden discovery, no mystification, no unexplained visual experience. The emblem is an integral part of the narrative subject, and though subject inevitably influences technique the effect is not pictorial, because of the passage's logical organization and the appearance of a gloss before the emblem.

Emblematic encounters similar to Scudamour's are far from rare in *The Faerie Queene*, and there are many other kinds of emblematic images in addition. In fact, Rosemary Freeman remarks in her important study of emblematic forms in Elizabethan literature that "the emblematic method is, in a greatly simplified way, Spenser's method." She then goes on to lay the foundations of some of the distinctions I am trying to make here: "Spenser's use of imagery is emblematic in the sense that the image and its significance are clearly distinguished from each other, and the likenesses are established point by point between them. These may be implicit rather than explicit, but there is no attempt at identification or fusion of the image with its object."[22] Freeman's illustration is from the *Daphnaida*:

> So all the world, and all in it I hate,
> Because it changeth euer too and fro,
> And neuer standeth in one certaine state,
> But still vnstedfast round about doth goe,
> Like a Mill wheele, in midst of miserie,
> Driuen with streames of wretchednesse and woe,
> That dying liues, and liuing still does dye.
>
> (428-434)

The simile in this passage presents an iconographic sign that

[22] *English Emblem Books*, pp. 101 and 103.

is not pictorial according to any of the criteria we have estab-
lished, but we may still recognize a familiar Spenserian pattern.
However, the main problems with Freeman's treatment of the
subject are, first, that her definition potentially encompasses
almost all similes and, second, that she does not keep images
and significances clearly separate.

A review of Freeman's reading of the *Prothalamion* will
show how easily the distinction between emblematic imagery
and the ordinary unfolding of allegory can be blurred. In this
case, the imprecision distorts our view of the poem's structure
because the swans are seen as emblematic throughout the
poem: "there is no elaborate series of comparisons by which
the swans are likened to the ladies but the image nevertheless
is emblematic from the beginning. In all the details of their
presentation the swans reflect the qualities and virtues of the
brides. A picture is made but it is not only a picture" (p. 104).
That is to say, the picture and the allegorical commentary
upon it are indistinguishable. The image is not a formally
discrete element of the poem, but seems to constitute the sum
of references to the swans throughout. This, in my opinion,
is not the case. The poem is emblematic because it contains a
precisely defined emblem which is followed by an elaborate
poetic embroidery in an allegorical action. The emblem—
which, defined more restrictively, also happens to be a Framed
image—is part of the allegorical development and explanation
in the same way that elements in an actual picture might be
part of a poem written beneath. In the *Prothalamion* the
emblematic Framed image and the allegory are clearly re-
lated but separate.

The stanza form of the *Prothalamion*, and especially the
refrain, establishes a series of discrete units inherently set off
from one another. The "action" of the lyric is somewhat more
disconnected than it might be in narrative, but still there is
a noticeable break when the appearance of the swans redirects

the formerly random activity of the nymphs. The Frame contains Focused imagery as well:

> With that I saw two Swannes of goodly hewe,
> Come softly swimming downe along the Lee;
> Two fairer Birds I yet did neuer see:
> The snow which doth the top of *Pindus* strew,
> Did neuer whiter shew,
> Nor *Ioue* himselfe when he a Swan would be
> For loue of *Leda*, whiter did appeare:
> Yet *Leda* was they say as white as he,
> Yet not so white as these, nor nothing neare;
> So purely white they were,
> That euen the gentle streame, the which them bare,
> Seem'd foule to them, and bad his billowes spare
> To wet their silken feathers, least they might
> Soyle their fayre plumes with water not so fayre,
> And marre their beauties bright,
> That shone as heauens light,
> Against their Brydale day, which was not long:
> Sweete *Themmes* runne softly, till I end my Song.
>
> (37-54)

Freeman's observation that the whiteness has "an ethical and aesthetic significance as well as a visual one" is correct, but her emphasis is misplaced when she says that "if the only point of all this is to establish that the swans are white, the method seems unnecessarily laboured" (p. 105). Poetic notions cannot be categorized in this way. For Spenser, to perceive the kind of whiteness for which he is trying to create a poetic image is simultaneously to perceive extraordinary virtue. One reason the image demands the allegorical exposition which follows it is that the extreme whiteness of the swans removes them from the realm of ordinary worldly birds, or even ordinary mythological birds. The point is not just to

establish that the birds are white, but that the full compre-
hension of their whiteness requires special perceptual and
metaphysical categories. The purpose of the Framed stanza
is to establish these categories: afterwards, the allegorical de-
velopment of action may proceed and emblematic details may
reappear. The importance of the lines about Leda and Jove
to the structure of the poem does not detract from their func-
tion in an attempted revelation of the swans' whiteness.
Neither of the pictorial techniques so far discussed can op-
erate to the exclusion of other poetic devices. Indeed, Focused
and Framed images almost inevitably have implications which
would have to be presented by other means in an actual picture.
It would be very difficult, if not impossible, to convey in a pic-
ture the ominous connotations of the comparison between
Acrasia's gown and Arachne's web; but this fact does not
diminish the visual impact of the verbal comparison. Spenser
does not create pictures; he makes images that are like pic-
tures in significant ways.

Some Framed Images

Perhaps digressions into modern prose and into a scene
from Shakespeare can usefully show that Framing is not ex-
clusively a feature of Spenser's eccentric style. In *Madame
Bovary*, when Emma receives the shattering letter from Ro-
dolphe, she dashes into a stiflingly hot attic, goes over to the
closed shutters of the dormer, and opens them:

la lumière éblouissante jaillit d'un bond.

En face, par-dessus les toits, la pleine campagne s'étalait
à perte de vue. En bas, sous elle, la place du village était
vide, les cailloux du trottoir scintillaient, les girouettes des
maisons se tenaient immobiles; au coin de la rue, il partit
d'un étage inférieur une sorte de ronflement à modulations
stridentes. C'était Binet qui tournait.

Elle s'était appuyée contre l'embrasure de la mansarde
et elle relisait la lettre avec des ricanements de colère.[23]

Flaubert presents only those few details that would be noticed
by a person looking at a familiar scene from an unusual
point of view, and Emma's action of throwing the shutters
open leads us to expect a scene framed in the opening. We
see this scene from a special and limited point of view, but
the few details, ordered as they are here, seem complete be-
cause of what we already know about the village. The image
is of a timeless and hypnotic void containing only the things
seized upon by Emma's distracted mind. Very quickly Emma
is almost drawn into the void, which seems to become an
active agent and to fuse her with itself. The image is not orna-
mental; it almost immediately becomes part of the scene's
action.

A comparison between the earlier and final versions of this
passage shows that selectivity and compression are important
to the effect of Framing, as of Focusing. Most of the deleted
material is no more than an explanation of things implied by
the context in the final version:

En face, par-dessus les toits des maisons, la pleine campagne
s'étalait à perte de vue et le soleil, s'allongeant sur les blés,
semblait épandre tout autour de lui dans les effluves de sa
couleur quelque chose d'immense et de désolé. En bas, à
pic sous elle, la place du village était vide. Le cailloutis

[23] (Paris: Editions Garnier Frères, 1961), p. 191; Francis Steegmul-
ler, trans. (New York, 1957), p. 231: ". . . the dazzling sunlight poured
in. Out beyond the roof-tops, the open countryside stretched as far as
eye could see. Below her the village square was empty; the stone side-
walk glittered; the weathervanes on the houses stood motionless. From
the lower floor of a house at the corner came a whirring noise with
strident changes of tone: Binet was at his lathe. Leaning against the
window frame she read the letter through, now and then giving an
angry sneer."

bleuâtre du trottoir scintillait, encadrant la terre qui était éblouissante de blancheur. On n'entendait rien, les girouettes des maisons se tenaient immobiles, s'était un silence universal et singulier, comme si tout ce qui vivait alors eût ensemble retenu sa respiration, dans quelqu'attente suprême. Tout à coup cependant, de l'étage inférieur d'une des maisons voisines, il partit au milieu de ce silence, comme un soupir de flûte ou une rafale de vent, une sorte de ronflement à modulations sourdes, tantôt hantes, tantôt basses. C'était Binet qui tournait.[24]

The organization of this early version is discursive, emphasizing the importance of the scene by explaining its parts. This discursiveness dilutes much of the scene's psychological effect, and Flaubert must mark the transition from stasis to action

---

[24] *Madame Bovary, nouvelle version précédée des scénarios inédits,* ed. Jean Pommier and Gabrielle Leleu (Paris: Librairie Jose Corti, 1949), pp. 442-443. Author's translation: Opposite, beyond the roofs of the houses, the open countryside stretched as far as the eye could see and the sun, lengthening across the grain, seemed to pour something boundless and desolate all around her in the streams of its color. Below, directly under her, the village square was empty. The bluish stones of the sidewalk glittered, framing the ground, whose whiteness was dazzling. Nothing was heard; the weathervanes on the houses stood motionless. There was a universal and remarkable stillness, as if all living things were then holding their breath together in some supreme anticipation. Suddenly, however, from the lower floor of one of the neighboring houses, out of the silence there began a whirring noise with muffled changes of tone, like the sigh of a flute or a burst of wind, now high, now low. Binet was at his lathe. There is an interesting later variation of the second sentence: "En bas, sous elle, le petit village, avec ses cours carrées et toutes ses jalousies closes, avait l'air enfoncé dans un silence de momie; la place était vide; son terrain blanchâtre éblouissait, et le bâtiment des halles, au milieu, y faisait comme une île sombre dans un lac de plomb," p. 443n. Author's translation: Below, beneath her, the small village with its square courts and all of its shades closed had an atmosphere sunken in the silence of death. The square was empty; its whitish surface was dazzling, and the market building in the middle seemed like a dark island there in a lake of lead.

with the emphatic "tout à coup." In the final version he places
the verb early in the sentence and achieves an effect similar
to that of "tout à coup" but more subtle. The verb alone re-
turns us again to temporality; the resumption of action is a
linguistic event which is lost in any English translation. Flau-
bert's revisions show a process of authorial withdrawal that
results in our perception of the Framed image as Emma per-
ceives it, and that enhances the effect when Emma is nearly
pulled into the hot, glittering void.[25]

We have been speaking mainly of Framed images which
present small spatial configurations. However, the treatment
of space in *Madame Bovary* can naturally lead us to an analy-
sis of larger spatial images in Shakespeare and Spenser. There
is a remarkable example of Framing in *King Lear,* when
Edgar leads Gloucester to a place the blinded man imagines
to be a cliff at Dover:

> Come on, sir; here's the place: stand still. How fearful
> And dizzy 'tis to cast one's eyes so low!
> The crows and choughs that wing the midway air
> Show scarce so gross as beetles; half way down
> Hangs one that gathers sampire, dreadful trade!
> Methinks he seems no bigger than his head.
> The fishermen that walk upon the beach
> Appear like mice, and yond tall anchoring bark
> Diminish'd to her cock, her cock a buoy
> Almost too small for sight. The murmuring surge,
> That on th'unnumber'd idle pebble chafes,
> Cannot be heard so high. I'll look no more,
> Lest my brain turn, and the deficient sight
> Topple down headlong.[26]

[25] For more commentary on this scene see Robert Martin Adams,
*Nil: Episodes in the Literary Conquest of Void during the Nineteenth
Century* (New York, 1966), Chapter Three, especially pp. 73-74.
[26] *The Arden Edition,* ed. Kenneth Muir (London, 1952), IV.vi.11-24.

Framing

Unlike descriptions of off-stage events spoken by characters like Enobarbus or Ariel, this passage is central to the action of the play. Those descriptions occur early in the plays, where they can serve to envelop a Cleopatra in sensuous atmosphere, or to secure our belief in the magical powers of a Prospero; the coloring they provide is important to all that follows, but not necessarily to any single event in the play. Edgar's picture of the view from the cliffs is different. It is directly linked to the action of the moment at which it appears; it interrupts that action, and the whole scene turns upon it. Shakespeare creates not only a visual effect but an illusion of space in this scene, the purpose of which is to convince Gloucester that he is standing on the brink of an abyss, and to convince the audience as well.

The scenic neutrality characteristic of Shakespeare's stage is analogous to the spacelessness of much of *The Faerie Queene*: in both instances neutral space may be transformed at any moment by language. There are no preconditions—no fixed stage sets, no established spatial framework—under which the action takes place.[27] Spaces are created *ad hoc* to suit the demands of the moment. In Spenser an example of this, which will be discussed later, is Britomart's encounter with the knights in front of the Castle Joyeous (3.1.20-22). The cliff scene from *King Lear* is more complex since the space pictured is a fiction within the fiction of the play. Shakespeare fuses these two levels of fiction for a moment so that the audience temporarily shares Gloucester's illusion of standing on a cliff. To be sure, Gloucester betrays some suspicion of the pretense when he complains "Methinks the ground is even"

---

[27] There was scenery of a kind on Shakespeare's stage, but we cannot be sure how or when it was used, and in any event Shakespeare never depends on it. Glynne Wickham terms the scenery of the period "emblematic"; see *Early English Stages 1300-1660, Volume Two: 1576 to 1660, Part I* (New York and London, 1963), pp. 206-275.

and says that he cannot hear the sea, but he is satisfied by Edgar's explanation, "Why, then your other senses grow imperfect/ By your eyes' anguish" (iv.vi.3-6). Because of the neutral character of Shakespeare's stage, the audience must accept Edgar's word until the dialogue resumes after Gloucester's imagined fall. Unlike the old man, we are at last disillusioned. But if the scene is staged on an open platform, as I think it was and should be, the audience is as much in the power of the poet as Gloucester is in the power of Edgar.

Edgar creates his illusion by calling attention to the perspective of the scene and by comparing things seen with things intellectually conceived. Perspective seems still to have been a novelty in Shakespeare's England: in "An Advertisement to the Reader" prefacing the illustrations to his translation of *Orlando furioso*, Sir John Harington says that "one thing is to be noted, which euery one (haply) will not obserue, namely the perspectiue in euery figure. For the personages of men, the shapes of horses, and such like, are made large at the bottome, and the fardest, shewes smallest, which is the chiefe art in picture."[28] The chief art in Edgar's picture is the orderly recession of its perspective, the extreme range of which is emphasized by the rapid shuttling back and forth between things perceived in distant space and things as they are known to be. Edgar's is a carefully structured and consistent spatial setting, attached by name to the geography of the real world and created specifically for an action that requires structure and consistency. Spenser, on the other hand, creates space to

---

[28] *Orlando Fvrioso in English Heroical Verse* (London, 1591), sig. A1 recto. But note that, according to Roy C. Strong, faint anticipations of the collecting vogue that was to arrive in England after about 1710 were beginning to appear at the close of Elizabeth's reign. See *The English Icon* (London and New York, 1969), p. 50. Perspective in painting thus cannot have remained a novelty for long; but Inigo Jones's first perspective stage settings created a sensation when Jonson's *Masque of Blacknesse* was presented at court in 1605.

contain events which will draw his characters into new adventures. In *King Lear*, as in certain Renaissance pictures, space becomes the subject. In *The Faerie Queene* the space is likely to be a *paysage moralisé* which reflects the events within it and exists only to contain them.

We may now return to *The Faerie Queene* for two last examples of Framing that will perhaps sharpen our definition. Britomart is about to enter the Castle Joyeous when this encounter occurs:

> At last as nigh out of the wood she came,
> A stately Castle farre away she spyde,
> To which her steps directly she did frame.
> That Castle was most goodly edifyde,
> And plaste for pleasure nigh that forrest syde:
> But faire before the gate a spatious plaine,
> Mantled with greene, it selfe did spredden wyde,
> On which she saw six knights, that did darraine
> Fierce battell against one, with cruell might and maine.

> Mainly they all attonce vpon him laid,
> And sore beset on euery side around,
> That nigh he breathlesse grew, yet nought dismaid,
> Ne euer to them yielded foot of ground
> All had he lost much bloud through many a wound,
> But stoutly dealt his blowes, and euery way
> To which he turned in his wrathfull stound,
> Made them recoile, and fly from dred decay,
> That none of all the sixe before, him durst assay.

> Like dastard Curres, that hauing at a bay
> The saluage beast embost in wearie chace,
> Dare not aduenture on the stubborne pray,
> Ne byte before, but rome from place to place,

To get a snatch, when turned is his face.
In such distresse and doubtfull ieopardy,
When *Britomart* him saw, she ran a pace
Vnto his reskew, and with earnest cry,
Bad those same sixe forbeare that single enimy.

(3.1.20-22)

Here, instead of a partly Framed emblem such as the shield
of Love (4.10.8), or a suspended Focused image such as that
of Britomart (4.6.20), the poet presents a space in which a
single action takes place, apparently unrelated to the main
narrative. The events Framed within the space are not ex-
plained until two stanzas later (3.1.24); indeed, the entire
episode in the Castle Joyeous is necessary to provide enlighten-
ment, even though we might call stanza twenty-four the
"Word" or explanation.[29] Like so many of the spaces in *The
Faerie Queene* this one is not part of a spatial continuum, and
it floats, suspended in the narrative, "plaste for pleasure nigh
that forrest syde."[30] Just as the "spatious plaine" remains un-

[29] I use the term "Word" to indicate all of the explanatory materials
surrounding an emblem. Poems often went with emblems and stood
under the picture; in actual emblem books the motto was often over
the picture.

[30] The space, for example, is not as carefully oriented for us as the
opening of *Piers Plowman* where, even though the dreamer is con-
fused, we do not necessarily feel that we are:

> Thanne gan I to meten   a merueilouse sweuene,
> That I was in a wildernesse   wist I neuer where,
> As I bihelde in-to the est   an hiegh to the sonne,
> I seigh a toure on a toft   trielich ymaked;
> A depe dale binethe   a dongeon there-inne,
> With depe dyches and derke   and dredful of sight.
> A faire felde ful of folke   fonde I there bytwene,
> Of alle maner of men   the mene and the riche,
> Worchyng and wandryng   as the worlde asketh.
> [B. Prologue, ll.11-19. *Piers the Plowman*, ed. Walter
> W. Skeat (Oxford, 1886), I.2]

explicated in terms of the poem's geography, the enigmatic action transpiring on it remains unintegrated into the main narrative of the poem until we finally proceed into the Castle Joyeous. This action, suspended in narrative time, is symmetrically disposed in the verbal time of stanza twenty-one around the ambiguously placed pluperfect clause in line five. The stanza is built antithetically around its core, and its structure belies our sense that these events exist in time. Just when the final line seems to suggest a definitive end to the brief narrative of holding off the six knights, Spenser fixes the entire scene for the reader with a simile that also carries a moral judgment. Only then does Britomart intervene. The Framed image implies Britomart's action, given her momentarily arrested presence in the main narrative—or, we might say, at the edge of this visual field.

Though it may be tempting to call this Framed image a "picture" because the simile "captures a moment," this stasis is possible only because the passage contains a complete seminal action. The simile absorbs this action and anticipates others by implication. The pictorial poet, like the painter, must understand phases of action and how we experience their visible unfolding. E. H. Gombrich has said that "just as music unfolds in phrases, so action unfolds in phases, and it is these units which are somehow the experienced moments in time, while the instant of which the theoreticians speak, the moment when time stands still, is an illicit extrapolation, despite the specious plausibility which the snapshot has given to this old idea.

"If we ask ourselves what quality a snapshot must possess to convey the impression of life and movement we will find, not unexpectedly, that this will again depend on the ease with which we can take in the meaning that allows us to supplement the past and arrive at an anticipation of the future."[31]

[31] "Moment and Movement in Art," *JWCI*, xxvii (1964), 303.

Some Framed Images

In the stanzas that show the "spatious plaine," we cannot be dealing literally with a *punctum temporis* since the stanzas themselves exist in time and, further, represent actions that take place in time; yet the effect is of a visually coherent whole that might once have been called a "point in time." Clearly this is one of those phases or "phrases" of action that makes sense if we stop it as it proceeds; Spenser has stopped his scene first by arranging it symmetrically in a stanza and then by employing a parallel simile.

As a final instance of Framing, let us take a passage from *The Faerie Queene* which is extensive enough to anticipate the technique of Scanning, the subject of the next chapter. Scudamour, traveling with Glauce and bent upon revenge against Britomart, is forced by night and a storm to seek a resting place. It turns out to be not very pleasant.

Not farre away, not meete for any guest
They spide a little cottage, like some poore mans nest.

Vnder a steepe hilles side it placed was,
There where the mouldred earth had cav'd the banke;
And fast beside a little brooke did pas
Of muddie water, that like puddle stanke,
By which few crooked sallowes grew in ranke:
Whereto approaching nigh, they heard the sound
Of many yron hammers beating ranke,
And answering their wearie turnes around,
That seemed some blacksmith dwelt in that desert ground.

There entring in, they found the goodman selfe,
Full busily vnto his worke ybent;
Who was to weet a wretched wearish elfe,
With hollow eyes and rawbone cheekes forspent,
As if he had in prison long bene pent:
Full blacke and griesly did his face appeare,
Besmeard with smoke that nigh his eye-sight blent;

With rugged beard, and hoarie shagged heare,
The which he neuer wont to combe, or comely sheare.

Rude was his garment, and to rags all rent,
Ne better had he, ne for better cared:
With blistred hands emongst the cinders brent,
And fingers filthie, with long nayles vnpared,
Right fit to rend the food, on which he fared.
His name was *Care*; a blacksmith by his trade,
That neither day nor night, from working spared,
But to small purpose yron wedges made;
Those be vnquiet thoughts, that carefull minds inuade.

(4.5.32-35)

The main action does not resume until two stanzas later when "Sir *Scudamour* there entring" is affected by Care; but a secondary action within the House of Care begins immediately. The pictorial effect is complete by the end of stanza thirty-five: two breaks in the action, the first at the beginning of the quoted passage and the second at the beginning of stanza thirty-four, create two pictorial moments. The first is a Framed image of the House of Care, which establishes a symbolic setting for the rest of the canto. Spenser shows no image of the House of Care from without, but simply mentions a "little cottage, like some poore mans nest." Instead, he presents a claustrophobic space which is the setting for Scudamour's allegorical tortures and which in retrospect symbolizes the almost psychotic introversion of the knight's jealousy. The House of Care is set into a hollow where a hillside has collapsed and it is closely bounded by a reed-lined stream. But our sense of spatial closure and constriction is heightened by the introverted ambiguities and puns of Spenser's language. The first two lines are intelligible only if we read "banke" to mean "hillside" (*OED*, 1.2.b); yet upon the appearance in the next line of a "little brooke" that is "fast beside" we cannot quite suppress the more familiar meaning of "banke," and the overlaid meanings of this word imply a spatial juxtaposition that verges upon superimposition. Finally, in a verbal tangle, the rhymed pun on "ranke" expresses closeness of atmosphere as closely demarcated space.

Especially considering the identical rhyme that links it to the image of the house, the sound of "many yron hammers beating ranke" might seem to be the Word under an Emblem; however, it is not clear what these hammers signify. It has been suggested that they are connected with the Furies as their origin is described by Boccaccio in the *Genealogia Deorum*. More likely, Spenser is embodying the metaphoric Italian idiom for jealousy, "martello d'amore," in a literal hammer image.[32] In any event, the suggestion that blacksmiths dwell here provides the background for the second pictorial moment, a Focused image of Care's face. The image is followed by a brief description of Care's clothes and hands before his identity is revealed. The last four lines of stanza thirty-five may be read as the "Word" standing under a combination of Framed and Focused images: the surroundings and appearance of the figure are embodied in images before we learn his name, and his name is merely part of an explanation of his significance. His trade tells us little more until we know what he makes, and we do not understand him fully until we see his exact role in the following action. The naming of such figures, as Rosemond Tuve says, "is not a great point; it is 'knowing' them rather than naming them that gives us trouble. Withholding the name often does intensify this pleasure in allegorical reading, in which identities and realities sometimes seem to dawn upon us like suns and then shine out."[33]

[32] See C. W. Lemmi, *Variorum*, 4.196, and John M. Steadman, "Spenser's House of Care: a Reinterpretation," *SRen*, VII (1960), 207-224.

[33] *Allegorical Imagery* (Princeton, 1966), p. 179.

Framing

Spenser's images typically do not reveal their whole significance even when they apparently are explained in the poem. If we associate Care and his apprentices with the Furies, or with the "martello d'amore," it is not so much because their iconographic significance is immediately manifest as because of what they do to Scudamour in the ensuing action. Almost invariably, we recognize the import of a figure in *The Faerie Queene* chiefly by his role as it unfolds, not by labels. Actions and signs in the poem usually support one another, and the strength of each is thereby increased; but our final understanding always comes through the development of the image or sign within the narrative. This is equally true whether the image is presented at the beginning of a phase of the fiction it dominates, as in the House of Care, or at the end, as in the appearance of Acrasia in the Bowre of Blisse. If this were not true, *The Faerie Queene* would be no more than a crude emblem book in words; such a book could not present us with a constantly engaging, coherently structured ordering of large moral and emotional issues.

CHAPTER FOUR

Larger Sights: Scanning

Both Focusing and Framing are primarily local, small in scale, and brief in duration. Scanning is broader, at once larger in scale and more diffuse. It exists in many forms and is more difficult to define than the other techniques, but we may say without exaggeration that Scanning is the Spenserian pictorial technique for which the other two are foundations. Spenser, as we have already seen, often imitates visual experience in divided and fractionalized imagery. He exploits the passage of verse-time in order to achieve a forceful display of phenomena that can be visualized in space or in imaginary tableaux. This process, which frequently governs the organization of larger sections of *The Faerie Queene* than we have been discussing, itself implies relative motion and is most apparent in passages involving movement. Therefore I divide Scanning into two basic varieties, according to types of motion. In the first, movement is from a distant and general view of a figure or scene to a closer view in which various details appear; in the second, motion is across or through a scene and different parts of it are encountered separately. The Cave of Mammon and the Bowre of Blisse are instances of the latter type of Scanning. The former is closer to techniques already explained in previous chapters; examples in Book One of *The Faerie Queene* include Arthur's appearance to Una and the approach to Lucifera's throne.

The essential quality of Scanning, observable in almost all of Spenser's set-pieces, is a process of shattering our impressions of Faerie Land into small, select fragments, reorganizing them and setting them beside one another in a vacuum, virtually against a background of gold leaf. The fragments may include Focusing and Framing in pure, diluted, or expanded forms, and—depending upon context—ordinary description as well; together, these elements sustain the powerful impression of Spenserian pictorialism. Not only may Scanning encompass Focusing and Framing, its structure is markedly similar to theirs: *The Faerie Queene* often presents persons or places in overlapping impressions which enrich our sensory, emotional, and intellectual perception of Faerie Land. Scudamour's approach to the House of Care has already illustrated this dynamic superimposition on a scale slightly large than that of the individual image. Another instance, to be discussed in this chapter, is the approach to the enthroned Lucifera (1.4.7ff.). Although there are no pure examples of Focusing in this passage, its effect is similar, on a large scale, to the brief impact of a Focused image. Likewise, passages in which Scanning is the main technique may show large-scale resemblances to Framed images, though no Framed images are included. Again, Lucifera is an example of this affinity, since our approach to the lady ends with naming her and explaining her identity (1.4.12).

Scanning is a halting, fragmenting process, but its progressive or cumulative nature is also important; for we must remember that analysis of pictorialism in literary works invokes analogies—not identities—with the cinema, the continuous narrative method in painting, or the process of our visual perception. The poet, unlike the painter, cannot present literally fixed images which refer to our past visual experience, depend on it, and extend it in fresh ways. To some extent all poetic images of quality represent the end of some process of visual discovery, but the pictorial poet employs rhetorical devices that emphasize the visual content of his imagery. However, the inherent and predetermined consecutiveness of poetry along with that explicitness of statement and connotation possible in words, makes the medium more systematic and in a sense more argumentative than purely visual art forms. Literary pictorialism thus cannot be understood as merely formal surface embellishment, since the pictorialist presents images in a vocabulary which shapes our responses. Lucifera, for example, is compared in a simile with Phaeton (1.4.9); she is surrounded with "sumptuous shew," likened to "the nourse of pompous pride," and has "scornefull feete" (1.4.7 and 10). A contrasting example, meant to invite approbation, is an image of extreme brightness that appears in the description of Arthur's shield three cantos later:

> all of Diamond perfect pure and cleene
> It framed was, one massie entire mould,
> Hewen out of Adamant rocke with engines keene,
> That point of speare it neuer percen could,
> Ne dint of direfull sword diuide the substance would.

> The same to wight he neuer wont disclose,
> But when as monsters huge he would dismay,
> Or daunt vnequall armies of his foes,
> Or when the flying heauens he would affray;
> For so exceeding shone his glistring ray,
> That *Phoebus* golden face it did attaint,
> As when a cloud his beames doth ouer-lay;
> And siluer *Cynthia* wexed pale and faint,
> As when her face is staynd with magicke arts constraint.

> (1.7.33-34)

Typically, Spenser defines the supernatural brilliance of the shield by comparing it precisely with two sights in nature. The shield is a natural paradox, bright enough to make the sun appear only a softened glow and to eclipse the moon entirely.[1] Though the poet may achieve pictorial effects, and

---

[1] "Attaint" and "stayned" should be taken in their early senses: "to touch . . . to hit in tilting" (*OED*, 1.1), and "to deprive of colour" or

by means analogous to those of cinema, painting, or our perceptual faculties, he almost inevitably accumulates commentary upon his pictures in the act of producing them.

Medieval and Renaissance Forms

In *Mimesis,* Eric Auerbach describes a more extreme variety of continuous subdivision of narrative sequence than we find in Spenser; the *Chanson de Roland* is his example of a medieval narrative which continually elaborates statements and actions by reiteration. The result is a shattering of experience—often into seemingly contradictory fragments which stand side by side. In his analysis of lines 737-780 of the *Chanson de Roland* (Oxford MS.), Auerbach says that "rationally organized condensations are avoided in favor of a halting, spasmodic, juxtapositive, and pro- and retrogressive method in which causal, modal, and even temporal relations are obscured." He goes on to relate the technique to epic "procedure": "Time and again there is a new start; every resumption is complete in itself and independent; the next is simply juxtaposed to it, and the relation between the two is often left hanging. This too is a type of epic retardation in Goethe's and Schiller's sense . . . but it is not managed through interpolations and episodes but through progression and retrogression within the principal action itself."[2] The technique of *Roland* almost approaches the character of a slide show. It would be an exaggeration to call *The Faerie Queene* a slide show, but the metaphor suggests Spenser's fixed concentration upon the distinct

---

"to throw into the shade by superior beauty or excellence" (*OED,* 1.a and b).

[2] *Mimesis,* Willard R. Trask, trans. (Princeton, 1953), p. 105. On Romanesque style in art and literature, including the *Chanson de Roland,* see D. W. Robertson, Jr., *A Preface to Chaucer* (Princeton, 1962), pp. 138-171. J. M. Evans, *Paradise Lost and the Genesis Tradition* (Oxford, 1968), pp. 155-156, discusses the use of an analogous narrative method in *Beowulf.*

parts of his visionary world as he constructs our experience of the whole.

The *Chanson de Roland* exemplifies Scanning in a lucid and striking form that is also employed by Spenser, who, like the *Roland* poet, often "strings independent pictures together like beads . . . . in such a fashion that, time and again, completely independent and self-contained scenes result" (p. 115). On the other hand, spaces between Spenser's richly elaborated scenes are usually undefined, whereas "the intervals in the *Chanson de Roland* are not always so very empty and flat; landscape sometimes intrudes; we see or hear armies riding through valleys and mountain passes" (p. 115). The blankness of the intervals in *The Faerie Queene* seems to heighten the richness of the places where our attention is concentrated, but still there is a kinship between the halting and involuted organization of *Roland* and the fractional treatment of experience in *The Faerie Queene*. In both poems verse-time is often not keyed to actions in the narrative, but becomes a medium for disposing events formally in space. These discrete clusters, frequently presented in complex detail and separated by gaps in narrative time that cause them to stand independently as coherent units, do not necessarily appear in logical order or in clear spatial or temporal relationship to each other.

Such discontinuities are familiar to most readers of *The Faerie Queene*. For example, when we lose sight of Redcrosse during Lucifera's progress out of the House of Pride (between 1.4.14 and 1.4.39), do we see the procession from Redcrosse's point of view, or does he see it at all? If he sees it, why does he remain in a place the moral danger of which is manifest? If he does not see it, why are we not told of his absence? We are not given enough information to be certain about all of the implications of the procession, yet the pageant itself is presented in lavish detail. We might well say of many moments in *The Faerie Queene* what Auerbach says of concretized gestures in the *Chanson de Roland*: "that the pictured scenes, in the impression they produce, closely approach the character of symbols or figures, even in cases where it is not possible to trace any symbolic or figural signification" (p. 116). We are tantalized by meanings which are not clearly revealed, and much of our uncertainty arises from the author's habit of treating some things in lavish detail and others hardly at all.

There are also differences between the two works. Spenser's method is closer to the usual epic procedure than is the *Roland* poet's, and his interest in the phenomenal world is definitely post-medieval. In the *Chanson de Roland*, where the author is almost exclusively concerned with the actions and words of a few characters, a "paratactic" narrative technique is primary, the poem's organization is very tight, and its European geography familiar. As Auerbach says, the subject "is narrow, and for the men who figure in it nothing of fundamental significance is problematic. All the categories of this life and the next are unambiguous, immutable, fixed in rigid formulations" (p. 110). *Roland* is governed almost entirely by predetermined concepts, not by encounters with immediate and problematic experience. By contrast, it is a cliché of Spenserian criticism that *The Faerie Queene* attempts virtually everything, and its cast of characters is vast. It is impossible to select a single "primary" technique from the huge variety of narrative and rhetorical techniques in Spenser's poem. Yet the real difference lies not so much in technique—though the number and complexity of techniques in *The Faerie Queene* is greater than in *Roland*—as in style in the broadest sense. Most important, encounters and struggles with the implicit assumptions of a poem like *Roland*, as well as with the complexities of the phenomenal world, are the very essence of *The Faerie Queene*. The two works are related much as fine medieval miniatures are related to paintings by the Renaissance masters: some of their methods may be similar—for example, placing several scenes from a narrative sequence in one picture panel—but the essence of Renaissance painting is different because of the artist's desire to harmonize his pictorial vision with experience of the surrounding visual world. What E. H. Gombrich says of the difference between medieval and post-medieval art is equally true of the difference between these two poems, even though both employ techniques which, at the most abstract level, are similar: "To the Middle Ages, the schema is the image; to the postmedieval artist, it is the starting point for corrections, adjustments, adaptations, the means to probe reality and to wrestle with the particular."[3]

The post-medievalism of Spenser's visual imagery is only one aspect of his syncretic approach to reality. His poem is omnivorous but, unlike Dante's and unlike the work envisioned in the Letter to Raleigh, not synthetic. The Letter reveals Spenser's ambition to encompass everything, but it scarcely hints that at the same time he will be searching for the scheme to contain it. Spenser does not feel obliged to proceed in any single way, and, besides the influence of court fashion and the great Italian poets of his century, his adoption of the Romance form reflects an evasion of constraint. "He chose a genre hospitable to varied kinds of opulence," as Rosemond Tuve has shown: "An astonishing accomplishment of Spenser's poem is that he makes one poetic whole for us without losing the intensely felt classical, or high Renaissance, or mediaeval character of materials so varied."[4] Perhaps explicable in this context is *The Faerie Queene*'s seemingly conventional and irrelevant opening stanza in which Spenser implicitly compares his own career with Virgil's before turning sharply about in the central line to echo Ariosto, indicating with no sense of incongruity that the poem is a Ro-

---

[3] *Art and Illusion*, 2nd ed. (Princeton, 1961), p. 173.
[4] *Allegorical Imagery* (Princeton, 1966), p. 383; Chapter Five, pp. 335-436, is on Spenser's use of Romance.

mance. Spenser seems at ease with the suggestion that he can combine the seriousness of Virgil and the scope of Ariosto within the framework of his chosen genre. He presents a work that is truly historical in conception, including, as it does within a literary framework drawn from the Middle Ages, elements of the Virgilian epic, classical mythology, religious allegory, Arthurian legend, Neoplatonic philosophy, and contemporary history. An important function of his visual imagery is to assert the actuality of each element of that heightened reality which he struggles to show precisely and to connect with action in our world.

The Nature of Scanning

W.B.C. Watkins in his essay "Spenser's Palace of Art" has, like Eric Auerbach, discovered ways of describing poetic procedure which help to define Scanning.[5] He tries to show Spenser's original treatment of the visual world by comparing the effects he achieves with those accomplished by various Western painters. However, Watkins is at his best when he breaks away from the history of art and begins to examine some of the extraordinary effects in *The Faerie Queene* from a more unusual point of view. He takes as his main example "the effect of light playing on a moving figure" in the scene in Book One when Una first sees Arthur moving toward her:

> A goodly knight, faire marching by the way
> Together with his Squire, arayed meet:
> His glitterand armour shined farre away,
> Like glauncing light of *Phoebus* brightest ray;
> From top to toe no place appeared bare,
> That deadly dint of steele endanger may:
> Athwart his brest a bauldrick braue he ware,
> That shynd, like twinkling stars, with stons most
>   pretious rare.

[5] *Shakespeare and Spenser* (Princeton, 1950), pp. 223-258.

And in the midst thereof one pretious stone
Of wondrous worth, and eke of wondrous mights,
Shapt like a Ladies head, exceeding shone,
Like *Hesperus* emongst the lesser lights,
And stroue for to amaze the weaker sights;
Thereby his mortall blade full comely hong
In yuory sheath, ycaru'd with curious slights;
Whose hilts were burnisht gold, and handle strong
Of mother pearle, and buckled with a golden tong.

(1.7.29-30)

The passage continues to celebrate Arthur at some length, but these lines with their progression from general to particular, show what Watkins means when he says that "Spenser gives a unique impression of the figure's moving forward. The pictorial becomes kinetic as only the camera, with its rapid succession of pictures, can capture pictorial movement; and this is accomplished not by saying in narrative that Arthur rides forward, but rather by shift of focus in visual imagery. Spenser may have hit upon this rare closeup by accident" (p. 252).

Watkins has virtually defined a kind of Scanning, and has used one of the richest sustained visual images in *The Faerie Queene* as his illustration. But why does he say that such a pictorial effect is "rare," that this instance may be an accident, when only a few pages before he has spoken at length about the sustained brightness of the image of Lucifera (1.4.6-12)? The two passages are similarly organized, except that Lucifera is observed by a moving eye whereas Arthur moves toward the observer. Without the contextual remarks to gloss the scene it might be difficult to say whether Arthur is approaching or being approached, but some sort of motion is involved and is clearly perceptible. In both passages the result is multiple overlapping images of the same object. Because Watkins takes the pictorialism of *The Faerie Queene* for granted and

is not seeking to formulate general definitions, he overlooks
the similarity between the two passages. As an example of
the "extraordinary . . . effect of light playing on a moving
figure" (p. 251), the approach of Arthur is ideal. It is prob-
ably the most sustained image of its type in the poem, but its
rarity depends upon accidental rather than essential qualities.
Watkins' formulation about this image can properly be gen-
eralized to cover others of comparable technique, especially
to include the effect of an observer moving toward an object.
As a brilliant and isolated *aperçu* describing a "rarity" in *The
Faerie Queene*, Watkins' observation may be admired as a
museum piece: it is also encouraging evidence that someone
else has observed and partly analyzed one of Spenser's pictorial
techniques, without extending that observation beyond a
single instance in the poem.

In his discussion of another stanza of the sequence detailing
Arthur's approach, Watkins continues his analogy with the
cinema. He says that the relatively low intensity possible in
any single poetic image is offset by rapid sequence in poetic
progression, and then adds that poetry's "pictorial effects in
time sequence can be made to dissolve so rapidly into others
that the actual series, unlike narrative panels in a triptych
or mural, is lost in an illusion of movement which has no
analogy until the discovery of movie fadeouts" (p. 254). This
is the example:

> Vpon the top of all his loftie crest,
> A bunch of haires discolourd diuersly,
> With sprincled pearle, and gold full richly drest,
> Did shake, and seem'd to daunce for iollity,
> Like to an Almond tree ymounted hye
> On top of greene *Selinis* all alone,
> With blossomes braue bedecked daintily;
> Whose tender locks do tremble euery one
> At euery little breath, that vnder heauen is blowne.

(1.7.32)

Here is something truly rare—not so much the rapid fading from one image into the next, already defined in Chapter Two as Focusing, but the attempt to capture the effect of complex motion. The other units (sometimes not a complete stanza) in this developing image of Arthur are fixed and self-contained; only the shift from one to another defines the movement, and we might say rather fancifully that the Arthur we see could be an elaborate statue being moved toward the observer in stages. Stanza thirty-two adds a second motion to the simple forward progression and brings the image of the prince to life. As I have said before, effects like this depend upon context, and upon what fragment of an impression they add to the particular image that has already been created. Watkins' choice of this passage seems to be based upon a strong but undefended feeling that it is pictorial. That he has been able to draw such rich generalizations from the scene is persuasive testimony to its pictorialism. However, let us consider the theoretical question directly and make some inquiries that arise naturally here but not in the context of Watkins' assumptions about Spenserian pictorialism.

First, how is the scene of Arthur's approach different from the famous description of Alcina in *Orlando furioso* (7.11-15): is the treatment of Arthur, like that of Alcina, not systematic and therefore different from the pictorial moments analyzed in previous chapters? Spenser's presentation is more orderly than the almost total randomness of normal perceptual sequence, but it does not proceed systematically.[6] This is not to say that disorder necessarily makes for pictorial poetry; a phenomenal order can exist where there is no governing logic or conceptual system. If logic ruled, we might move in order from an overall view of Arthur to his "loftie crest," "haughtie

---

[6] James J. Gibson, *The Perception of the Visual World* (Boston, 1950), pp. 12-25, "Theories of Perception," *et passim*; and M. D. Vernon, *The Psychology of Perception* (Baltimore, 1962), especially pp. 31-39, "The Perception of Objects by Adults."

helmet," "bauldrick braue," "warlike shield," "mortall blade," and then to his history. In fact, Spenser moves from a general view to the baldric, the jewel upon it, the sword, helmet, crest, shield, and then to the history. This order is partly determined by rhetorical emphasis, since the shield is the most remarkable piece of Arthur's equipment and properly should come last. But the shield happens to be covered, and is therefore the least visible of Arthur's effects; since it is covered, it needs explanation, and the account naturally leads into the history. The sequence of the other stanzas (1.7.29-32) is less easy to explain unless we recognize that they are ordered to imitate the perceptual effect of Scanning an approaching figure. Thus, as Arthur approaches, we get both finer and more extensive detail: the baldric receives seven lines, devoted almost entirely to establishing that it "shynd, like twinkling stars"; the sword is "ycaru'd with curious slights," and we see that its "hilts were burnisht gold, and handle strong/ Of mother pearle, and buckled with a golden tong" (1.7.30); and the helmet is given a full stanza of lavish detail. Finally, the crest alone receives a stanza (1.7.32), and along with its exquisite refinements we can see the slightest movement.

Many of my earlier remarks about the importance of context to pictorialism apply to this passage, where Focused imagery not only helps to establish motion but contributes directly to the pictorial effect. Any similar presentation showing Arthur's movement toward Una would probably be pictorially suggestive, but Spenser's pictorialism is doubly impressive because he embellishes the basic motion with effects that enhance its latent qualities.[7] The seven lines on the baldric (1.7.29-30) have many of the qualities of a Focused image,

---

[7] When Marlowe transposes this stanza into blank verse in the context of a set speech imagining triumph, it remains visually striking despite Tamburlaine's interjection to explain his own symbolism (*Tamburlaine II*, 2.4.3).

except that the lines, "Like *Hesperus* emongst the lesser lights,/ And stroue for to amaze the weaker sights," return, in a more detailed version, to the constellation image by which the jewels on the baldric are first defined. Arthur's crest (1.7. 32) is even closer to being a Focused image. Stanza thirty-one in particular shows the importance of contextual development to Scanning. The stanza is bounded by the two passages on Arthur that we have just discussed, but these lines are loosely organized although they offer quite a lot of visual information. For a number of lines Spenser sustains precise control over the visual impact of his verse without employing strictly Framed or Focused images:

> His haughtie helmet, horrid all with gold,
> Both glorious brightnesse, and great terrour bred;
> For all the crest a Dragon did enfold
> With greedie pawes, and ouer all did spred
> His golden wings: his dreadfull hideous hed
> Close couched on the beuer, seem'd to throw
> From flaming mouth bright sparkles fierie red,
> That suddeine horror to faint harts did show;
> And scaly tayle was stretcht adowne his backe full low.
>
> (1.7.31)

In itself the stanza is a catalog, but in context it adds considerably to the pictorialism of the sequence. Spenser notes that the helmet "great terrour bred," and then shifts his point of view in order to observe the approaching helmet. It is the sight that breeds terror, for the object is at a distance and its fierceness is largely self-contained: the "Dragon did enfold/ With greedie pawes, and ouer all did spred/ His golden wings." The fire "did *show*" horror (italics mine), but the Dragon's threatening liveliness is contained as the eye passes on to the "scaly tayle," which is placed epigrammatically to remind us of the

Dragon's position in Arthur's attire as well as its serpentine quality.

Stanza thirty-one is imitated from Tasso, and Spenser's changes help us to realize the delicate adjustments of which his pictorial art is capable:

> Porta il Soldan su l'elmo orrido e grande
> serpe che si dilunga e il collo snoda,
> su le zampe s'inalza e l'ali spande
> e piega in arco la forcuta coda.
> Par che tre lingue vibri e che fuor mande
> livida spuma, e che 'l suo fischio s'oda.
> Ed or ch'arde la pugna, anch'ei s'infiamma
> nel moto, e fumo versa insieme e fiamma.
>
> (9.25)

> High on the Soldan's helm enamell'd laid
> A hideous dragon, arm'd with many a scale,
> With iron paws, and leathern wings display'd,
> Which twisted in a knot her forked tail;
> With triple tongue . . . she hiss'd and bray'd;
> About her jaws the froth and venom trail,
> And as he stirr'd, and as his foes him hit,
> So flames to cast and fire she seem'd to spit.

Tasso is chiefly interested in symbolic action, and this brief description is suspended in an account of an attack by the Soldan. Nor is the stanza an arbitrarily placed ornament to the main action, since the dragon on the helmet actually participates in the battle: "Ed or ch'arde la pugna, anch'ei s'infiamma/ nel moto, e fumo versa insieme e fiamma." The helmet is a significant element of the Soldan's fierceness—not an object, but an active agent. Although Spenser's description of Arthur's helmet is similar to the lines from Tasso, Arthur's helmet remains an object upon which the viewer may project significance. Spenser is interested not so much in making the helmet function in the action of the poem as in defining an impression of its appearance; the helmet does nothing, but "*seem'd* to throw/ From flaming mouth bright sparkles fierie red" (italics mine).

Spenser's tendency to isolate objects from the main action and to dwell upon them is nowhere more apparent than in this comparison with Tasso.[8] Spenser encloses his description of Arthur's helmet with accounts of objects strangely distant from the observer, and he paradoxically contrasts its effect with its actual inertness. Instead of leaving the end of his description open in order to link it with what follows as Tasso does, Spenser concludes his account of the relation between observer and object with one descriptive detail; thus, the line "And scaly tayle was stretcht adowne his backe full low" closes off the stanza and isolates it from what comes after. This arrangement of descriptive materials set in the formally closed context of the surrounding stanzas heightens the pictorialism of these particular lines by contributing to our impression of fragmented visualization. An important purpose of the rhetoric of *The Faerie Queene* is to make Faerie Land vivid, but to place it just out of reach; to allow us to understand it in our own terms, but also to make us realize that it is distant and very special. Scanning fulfills this purpose, if we may call it a rhetorical technique, for it simultaneously achieves pictorial vividness and calls attention to formal di-

---

[8] Galileo objected to Tasso's narrative style on the grounds that it was fragmented ("intarsiata") compared with Ariosto's; he particularly objected to the distortions of narrative brought about by Tasso's allegorical intentions. It is probably true that the styles of both Spenser and Tasso are fragmented in contrast to Ariosto's, but Spenser goes far beyond Tasso. See Erwin Panofsky, *Galileo as a Critic of the Arts* (The Hague, 1954), pp. 13-20. Panofsky cites Galileo's "Considerazioni al Tasso," *Scritti letterari*, ed. Alberto Chiari (Florence, 1943), p. 87.

visions and arrangements. It combines the pictorial with the iconic, descriptive, and emblematic. Tasso's narrative style is complicated yet smooth compared with Spenser's, and it allows the reader to be drawn into the action; narrative suspense and the illusionism that makes it possible arise out of an art which does not assert itself so boldly as Spenser's does in *The Faerie Queene*. Spenser uses pictorial energy rather than the energy of suspense to hold his reader's attention and heighten his awareness.

We have so far been concerned with a variety of Scanning in which pictorial images and description arising from one object and its immediate surroundings overlap to form a composite impression. This shifting accretion of fragmented images is best understood as a broad expansion of Focusing. The effect of Scanning is most obvious when either the object itself or the point of observation is moving, and when increasing richness of image is reinforced by an increasing awareness of the image's meaning (as we shall see in the approach to Lucifera). Nonetheless, the essential element of the technique is the shattering of perceptual experience into a sequence of relatively small and concentrated units; such a sequence almost inevitably implies motion. The units may have a formally explicable order like those arranged in an understandable—not necessarily logical—relation to one another in many paintings employing the continuous narrative method.[9] The effect of Scanning can be exaggerated by relative motion between observer and object; converging, diverging, or lateral motion can clarify the effect of repeated and varying perceptions the order of which is mimetic of, if not

---

[9] "Continuous narration" in which successive narrative events are shown in a single picture is a familiar technique in medieval art. See Kurt Weitzmann, "Narration in Early Christendom," *American Journal of Archaeology*, LXI (1957), 83-91.

identical with, our scanning and classification of the visual world.

The passage in which Calidore comes upon Mount Acidale exemplifies the close relationship between Scanning in its rudimentary form and Focusing. Calidore watches the scene from "the couert of the wood":

> There he did see, that pleased much his sight,
> That euen he him selfe his eyes enuyde,
> An hundred naked maidens lilly white,
> All raunged in a ring, and dauncing in delight.

> All they without were raunged in a ring,
> And daunced round; but in the midst of them
> Three other Ladies did both daunce and sing,
> The whilest the rest them round about did hemme,
> And like a girlond did in compasse stemme:
> And in the middest of those same three, was placed
> Another Damzell, as a precious gemme,
> Amidst a ring most richly well enchaced,
> That with her goodly presence all the rest much graced.

> Looke how the Crowne, which *Ariadne* wore
> Vpon her yuory forehead that same day,
> That *Theseus* her vnto his bridale bore,
> When the bold *Centaures* made that bloudy fray
> With the fierce *Lapithes*, which did them dismay;
> Being now placed in the firmament,
> Through the bright heauen doth her beames display,
> And is vnto the starres an ornament,
> Which round about her moue in order excellent.

> Such was the beauty of this goodly band,
> Whose sundry parts were here too long to tell:
> But she that in the midst of them did stand,
> Seem'd all the rest in beauty to excell,

Crownd with a rosie girlond, that right well
Did her beseeme. And euer, as the crew
About her daunst, sweet flowres, that far did smell,
And fragrant odours they vppon her threw;
But most of all, those three did her with gifts endew.

(6.10.11-14)

In this scene the subject is a closed phrase or phase of action
in which motion is implied but not represented;[10] the scene,
like so many others in *The Faerie Queene*, is set into the nar-
rative as if it were a subjectively observed picture in which
motion is suggested but is not actually imitated as it is in the
lines showing Arthur's approach. The pattern of the image
is the familiar one of statement, elaboration, and restatement;
as the observations overlap, the image increases in visual com-
plexity through a process of qualification and correction. Thus,
"maidens . . ./ All raunged in a ring" is modified in the next
stanza to "All they without were raunged in a ring." The re-
peated words emphasize that this is a correction: in fact there
are three ladies inside the ring, about whom the others "like
a girlond did in compasse stemme," and set in the middle of
the two rings "another Damzell, as a precious gemme." The
simile that makes up stanza thirteen is more abstract and
reaches intellectually into a distant mythological past, which,
because of the conflation of two myths, is made to seem even
more distant and confused in a kind of aerial perspective.[11]
The syntax partly conceals a break where the last two lines
add an emblem parallel to the original image; these lines ex-
plain the simile's abrupt opening instruction to look at an

---

[10] For a discussion of ways in which closed phases of action are
shown in pictures see E. H. Gombrich, "Moment and Movement in
Art," *JWCI*, xxvii (1964), 303-306. In *The Poetry of The Faerie Queene*,
pp. 12-14, Paul J. Alpers discusses the pictorialism of Calidore's vision
using terms entirely different from mine.
[11] See *Variorum*, 6.249-251.

unsupplied image: "Looke how the Crowne, which *Ariadne* wore/ Vpon her yuory forehead that same day." The simile is an emblem turned inside out or upside down: the first seven lines are the poem accompanying and explaining the emblem —stars in the figure of a crown that "is vnto the starres an ornament,/ Which round about her moue in order excellent." The next stanza reminds us again of the central figure, "crownd with a rosie girlond." Finally, we move back to the dancing ladies who are throwing flowers on the garlanded figure, now also crowned by much-embellished images and emblems.

The similarities between this image of the dancers and Graces and Focused images defined earlier are evident; however, unlike Focused images, this one does not concentrate upon a single visual phenomenon, but upon a closed phase of observed action which can be emblematically fixed. The visual intensity of the image is decreased by the rather abstract emblematic simile, although the mythologically distant intricacies of this simile and its forceful opening, "Looke how the Crowne, which *Ariadne* wore," do support the visual force of its ending. The ending, which is a transition to the last of the three stanzas containing the image, sustains the original vision of circling "in order excellent." The mosaic effect of Calidore's vision scene brings it close to Focusing, yet the scene is not Focused because of its diffuseness; its larger scale and fragmented organization make it an example in miniature of Scanning. Focusing is limited to the rendering of individual and very particular visual phenomena, whereas Scanning can represent entire scenes.

Approaching Lucifera

Few of the examples discussed in the chapters on Focusing and Framing come from the great set-pieces in *The Faerie Queene* because it seemed desirable to show first that the pictorialism of *The Faerie Queene* is pervasive and not confined to these set-pieces alone. Moreover, to describe the relation of passages in the set-pieces which employ Focusing and Framing to their elaborately descriptive and iconographic surroundings is to define the technique of Scanning itself. The presence of isolated pictorial moments does not alone explain the force of Spenserian pictorialism. It is no accident that Spenser's set-pieces attract the attention of writers who attempt to analyze his pictorial vividness, for in these pieces we find intensely pictorial passages embedded in and supported by other visual materials which are more loosely organized. As the instance of Arthur's helmet shows, the effect of pictorial moments tends to splash over and to make juxtaposed passages, which in isolation would properly be called descriptive, seem more vivid. Our impression in the set-pieces is of a much more extensive pictorialism than a rigid application of previous definitions might indicate, and removing the few strictly pictorial images from *The Faerie Queene* would radically change its nature. These images sustain and vivify a far greater bulk of descriptive, emblematic, and iconic material. Spenser combines pictorial images with masses of material having some visual reference. Differently treated visual materials support one another and pictorial details energize the whole.

The approach to Lucifera in Book One of *The Faerie Queene* is an excellent example of the first type of Scanning and of the intensification of the visual effect of nonpictorial materials by their context. The stanzas on Lucifera include Framed and Focused imagery combined with descriptive materials and moral judgments carried by images. This type of Scanning, which shows the observer and the object he observes converging, has already been partly illustrated by my remarks on Watkins' treatment of our first view of Arthur. We approach Lucifera through a series of light-drenched images which accumulate to make the whole passage glitter. Gradually we move on to the lady's background, and finally her significance, which is summed up by the revelation of her name:

Arriued there they passed in forth right;
For still to all the gates stood open wide,
Yet charge of them was to a Porter hight
Cald *Maluenù*, who entrance none denide:
Thence to the hall, which was on euery side
With rich array and costly arras dight:
Infinite sorts of people did abide
There waiting long, to win the wished sight
Of her, that was the Lady of that Pallace bright.

By them they passe, all gazing on them round,
And to the Presence mount; whose glorious vew
Their frayle amazed senses did confound:
In liuing Princes court non euer knew
Such endlesse richesse, and so sumptuous shew;
Ne *Persia* selfe, the nourse of pompous pride
Like euer saw. And there a noble crew
Of Lordes and Ladies stood on euery side,
Which with their presence faire, the place much
    beautifide.

High aboue all a cloth of State was spred,
And a rich throne, as bright as sunny day,
On which there sate most braue embellished
With royall robes and gorgeous array,
A mayden Queene, that shone as *Titans* ray,
In glistring gold, and peerelesse pretious stone:
Yet her bright blazing beautie did assay
To dim the brightnesse of her glorious throne,
As enuying her selfe, that too exceeding shone.

Scanning

Exceeding shone, like *Phoebus* fairest childe,
That did presume his fathers firie wayne,
And flaming mouthes of steedes vnwonted wilde
Through highest heauen with weaker hand to rayne;
Proud of such glory and aduancement vaine,
While flashing beames do daze his feeble eyen,
He leaues the welkin way most beaten plaine,
And rapt with whirling wheels, inflames the skyen,
With fire not made to burne, but fairely for to shyne.

So proud she shyned in her Princely state,
Looking to heauen; for earth she did disdayne,
And sitting high; for lowly she did hate:
Lo vnderneath her scornefull feete, was layne
A dreadfull Dragon with an hideous trayne,
And in her hand she held a mirrhour bright,
Wherein her face she often vewed fayne,
And in her selfe-lou'd semblance tooke delight;
For she was wondrous faire, as any liuing wight.

Of griesly *Pluto* she the daughter was,
And sad *Proserpina* the Queene of hell;
Yet did she thinke her pearelesse worth to pas
That parentage, with pride so did she swell,
And thundring *Ioue*, that high in heauen doth dwell,
And wield the world, she claymed for her syre,
Or if that any else did *Ioue* excell:
For to the highest she did still aspyre,
Or if ought higher were then that, did it desyre.

And proud *Lucifera* men did her call,
That made her selfe a Queene, and crownd to be,
Yet rightfull kingdome she had none at all,
Ne heritage of natiue soueraintie,

But did vsurpe with wrong and tyrannie
Vpon the scepter, which she now did hold:
Ne ruld her Realme with lawes, but pollicie,
And strong aduizement of six wisards old,
That with their counsels bad her kingdome did vphold.

Soone as the Elfin knight in presence came,
And false *Duessa* seeming Lady faire,
A gentle Husher, *Vanitie* by name
Made rowme, and passage for them did prepaire:
So goodly brought them to the lowest staire
Of her high throne, where they on humble knee
Making obeyssance, did the cause declare,
Why they were come, her royall state to see,
To proue the wide report of her great Maiestee.

(1.4.6-13)

The quoted passage is immediately preceded by a Framed image of the palace, covered with "golden foile," in which the lady lives (1.4.4). This famous image of spurious architectural display establishes the skeptical attitude toward appearances with which we are to approach Lucifera, and the "Word" or explanation underneath (1.4.5) characterizes the place explicitly by revealing things the eye cannot see as it approaches: that the palace is built upon a "sandie hill," that "euery breath of heauen shaked it," and that "all the hinder parts, that few could spie,/ Were ruinous and old, but painted cunningly."[12] The beginning of our quotation articulates a second phase of the action. The name of the porter *Maluenù* helps further to establish for the reader, though not for Redcrosse, the undesirability of this palace as a resort. Stanza six is neutral and

---

[12] For a discussion of the iconography of the image see A. C. Hamilton, *The Structure of Allegory in The Faerie Queene* (Oxford, 1961), p. 67.

vague in point of pictorial qualities; it names visible things in order, but does not perceive them for us. Scanning can absorb description, but it is pictorial because it imitates synthetic processes of visualization—not because it mimics the registration of visible things on the retina. Stanza seven opens with another articulation of action, and the approach to Lucifera begins. However, we do not see the approach simply from Redcrosse's point of view, though we appear sometimes to be following him. The sudden shifts of perspective and interpolated explanations cannot be his. That the passage represents an approach to the "Presence" seems clear, since stanza seven decisively begins the action, and thirteen, which opens with "Soone as the Elfin knight in presence came," shows the company brought "to the lowest staire/ Of her high throne." "Presence" suggests something divine or holy, but even at this early stage the reader senses that the suggestion is inappropriate; and the rhyme of "shew" with "crew," by emphasizing these words, strengthens his feeling of suspicion. Stanza seven provides the general framework for what follows and establishes the voluptuousness of the court, which "Ne *Persia* selfe, the nourse of pompous pride/ Like euer saw."

Stanzas eight through ten are the pictorial core of the entire scene. Stanza eight is almost a Focused image in itself; however, the last three lines, instead of continuing the accumulation of images, revert to a rational order of comparison. Still, the visual effect is powerful, in part because of the preparation in stanza seven, but also because the concentration upon a massed brightness—"gorgeous array," "*Titans* ray," "glistring gold, and peerelesse pretious stone"—fuses the eye to "her bright blazing beautie," while the syntactically ambiguous "that" at the stanza's center fixes our attention for a moment on the brightness of its two antecedents. W.B.C. Watkins, whose general thesis is that Spenser anticipates many visual effects found only in later painting, describes the effect of this brightness well: "Such intensity and variety of glittering light is not paralleled on canvas until painters begin to break up pigment to secure color vibration. . . . In Spenser's portrait Lucifera is *featureless*, very much like Monet's disembodied cathedral façades, where the substance of structure seems to melt under the light playing over its surface."[13] One qualification is that the light, more than playing over the surface, it generated by it.

Stanza nine, one of Spenser's finest similes, is the pivotal image in the approach to Lucifera. This stanza is so closely linked to the preceding one by the repetition of "exceeding shone," and by the elaboration of a comparison with the Sun already begun with the reference to "*Titans* ray," that the two function as a unit. The elements of that unit are antithetical, and together they demonstrate the shattering effect of Scanning. Stanzas eight and nine are formally discrete units that are allied linguistically yet also represent two different narrative points of view. In 1758 John Upton observed, "Tis a very elegant figure our poet here uses, to correct himself with a repetition of the same words. He had compared Pride to Titan or to the Sun; correcting himself he adds, or rather this emblem of the world's vanity is to be compared to Phaeton, the Sun's false representative."[14] Upton singles out the essential relationship between the two stanzas, but the modern reader may well go on to ask who is correcting whom. There is more than self-correction and amplification here—the disjunction between the stanzas is as radical as their superficial rhetorical and logical relationship is powerful.

Stanza nine announces itself in the first line as a correction of what has gone before; it is like an aside spoken in a play by a particularly credible character who steps out to interpret

[13] *Shakespeare and Spenser*, p. 251.
[14] *Variorum*, 1.214-215. Brooke, *Variorum*, 1.215, says that this figure is used only fourteen times in *The Faerie Queene*.

an event for the audience. In stanza eight Lucifera's bright-
ness is dazzling, and the simile that follows reveals its cause:
the brightness is as deviant and unnatural as the sun-chariot
driven off its course by Phaeton. Here the speaker is correcting
not himself, but rather the perceptions of a naive eye as it
approaches the "Presence." The shattering of point of view
can be morally as well as visually functional: this simile de-
velops the visual implications of an immediately preceding
image, and also reinterprets that image by constructing an-
other which is still more forceful. In this passage the contin-
uing enrichment of the visual impression through juxtaposed
images is accompanied by an ever increasing pressure toward
moral judgment which culminates in the naming of the
"Queene." In every sense, we see more and more clearly as
we proceed. These lines occur not only at the pictorial core
of the scene, but at a decisive moral juncture. The image of
the House of Pride, the name of the porter, and the vocabu-
lary surrounding the "Presence" all influence our judgment,
but the simile unquestionably confirms the evil and disruptive
character of Lucifera. The unmistakable kinship between
Phaeton's story and Lucifer's fall leads us to understand the
lady's infernal connections before we learn her parentage and
name. The idea of the false as a parody of the true echoes
throughout the passage, beginning with the image of the
House of Pride and continuing very strongly with the Phae-
ton image. As Kathleen Williams says, "only in the heavenly
city can excessive light exist without blame. Lucifera's palace
is, like Milton's hell, an imitation of heaven, its excess of
glory is a sin of extreme gravity."[15] Finally, at the close of

---

[15] *Spenser's World of Glass* (Berkeley and Los Angeles, 1966), p. 13.
Williams observes that "in *Apelles Symbolicus* the fall from the
sun chariot is confidently glossed: 'In Luciferum aliosque rebelles
Angelos e coele dejectos.'"

Approaching Lucifera

Book One we catch an authentic glimpse of the heavenly city
when Una's veil is drawn away and she emerges:

> As bright as doth the morning starre appeare
> Out of the East, with flaming lockes bedight,
> To tell that dawning day is drawing neare,
> And to the world does bring long wished light.
>
> (1.12.21)

The accumulating pressure of judgment against Lucifera is
important to the total effect of her appearance, but it might
be said that the first line of stanza nine alone would be suffi-
cient to increase this pressure and that the rest of the stanza
is ornamental pictorialism for its own sake. This is not the
case, for Spenser's image sustains the moral statement by
showing the exact, dangerous character of Lucifera's bright-
ness; she is like Phaeton at a particular, most blazing, and
threatening moment of his history. The simile is an icono-
graphically precise moral commentary as well as a link in
the chain of images of brightness begun in stanza eight. That
part of the Phaeton myth selected for representation in this
simile is the pivotal action, one that has been chosen as a sub-
ject by many artists, including Michelangelo. The image of
Phaeton disordered, running out of control close to the earth,
epitomizes his weakness, pride, and destructiveness; further,
the image is iconographically linked with the parallel fall
of Lucifer, whereas an image of a young man either soaring
in a grand chariot before the fall or shattered afterwards would
provide no clear sign for identification. The distinguishing
features of both stories are the falling through mid-air and
the accompanying disorder. Spenser is careful to present Phae-
ton at the moment when "He leaues the welkin way most
beaten plaine,/ And rapt with whirling wheels, inflames the
skyen." But one might argue that Spenser's image is abstract,

and not at all a visual presentation of disorder: indeed "rapt with whirling wheels" may seem abstract if "rapt" is taken to mean "enthralled," "entranced," or even "swept away by" the moving wheels of the chariot. Since Phaeton is entranced by his own illusory power and is unable to control the chariot, this is obviously one of the intended meanings; but another (*OED*, III.8) is that Phaeton is enveloped or engulfed by the wheels—that they actually pull him into themselves as his chariot distintegrates. A similar double usage of the word appears later in *The Faerie Queene*, as Guyon and the Palmer approach "that perilous Poole,"

> That called was the *Whirlepoole of decay*,
> In which full many had with haplesse doole
> Beene suncke, of whom no memorie did stay:
> Whose circled waters rapt with whirling sway,
> Like to a restlesse wheele, still running round,
> Did couet, as they passed by that way.
>
> (2.12.20)

Read in a parallel way, the visual element in the Phaeton simile is undeniably strong, even though lines two through five are no more than a setting for the scene pictured in its last four lines. This kind of arrangement in a simile is common enough, but in general it dilutes pictorial effects by emphasizing the intellectual order of a comparison rather than its character as a visual image. In this particular case, however, pictorial forcefulness is preserved because in context the simile does not illustrate an abstraction but serves to amplify a statement already made in largely pictorial terms. The reader will recall an opposite arrangement in the simile recounting Britomart's approach to the Castle Joyeous (3.1.22). That simile contains a closed phrase of action which is already implicit in its first line and a half—"Like dastard Curres, that hauing at a bay/ The saluage beast" (3.1.22). In part, this image's economical structure is possible because it alludes to a familiar kind of incident; but equally important is that the essential action is stated first and elaborated later.

Stanza ten, which resumes the approach to Lucifera, parallels Arthur's approach in adding to the basic image of dazzling light details seen close up: a dragon is at the feet of the "Queene" and a "mirrhour bright" reflects her own brightness back into itself. In itself this stanza does little more than name iconographic signs, but combined with what has gone before it continues and reinforces the pictorialism of the entire passage. Stanzas eleven and twelve explain the image of Lucifera. We learn of her gloomy parentage, her name, which itself constitutes her significance, and we are given a full summary of her ambitions. These two stanzas stand beneath the multiple and overlapping images representing the approach to Lucifera like the "Word" beneath an emblem; they explain significances already implicit in the image as it has been unfolded, and seem to be overt guidance from that voice which has been pressing us to moral judgment throughout the approach.

The construction of this mosaic of Lucifera is analogous, on a large scale, to that of Focused and Framed passages analyzed above. Although no single stanza is rigorously pictorial, stanzas eight and nine at the core of the passage come very close to it in themselves, and taken in their context present overlapping images of brightness the visual impact of which is considerable. The effectiveness of the composite image may be accounted for in several ways. Chief among these is the concentration on Lucifera's brightness: while no comprehensive description is given of the "Queene," attention is exclusively concentrated on her. On the one hand, intervening judgments and explanations weaken the effect of visual information; on the other, concentrated attention on one phenomenon counteracts the dilution. Our illusion of actually approaching Lucifera further enhances the total pictorial effect of the extended imagery. There is continuous elaboration of the original image by the additional images imposed upon it as we approach the throne.

Spenser can afford this apparent squandering of poetic resources because his image of Lucifera with the explanation or "Word" beneath it *is* her nature. The entire image, Framed in action with its gloss, is all that is essential to our understanding of why she is evil. One of Spenser's reasons for withholding Lucifera's name until the last is surely to allow his readers to arrive at their own understanding of her nature before he clinches the identification. The naming is more ritualistic than revelatory, and our satisfaction more at confirmation than at discovery. We have been forced into a test, and must ask ourselves whether we would kneel before Lucifera along with Redcrosse. To say that we would not is subtly to participate in her pride, but to realize that we should not is essential to accurate reading. The intensity of Lucifera's brightness is the correlative of her insidious evil; both are dazzling and attractive, and Spenser does not refrain from making them seem so. In order to be a convincing threat, the image must be so pictorially forceful that only a similar image can control our understanding of it—this is the function of the Phaeton simile. Only in this way can Spenser lead his audience to a full realization of Lucifera's dangerous hypnotic powers.

Interior Space in the Cave of Mammon

In many ways the first variety of Scanning, which has so far been the main study of this chapter, is severely limited; explicitly or implicitly, it involves an observer moving toward a fixed object, person, or scene, or an object or person moving toward a fixed observer. Such motion is rendered in broken, overlapping, perceptual fragments which together make up what we call the scene or image. In the simplest example discussed above, Calidore's view of the dance on Mount Acidale, there is no converging motion, but linked images which imitate the eye's discovery of more and more about what confronts it. The eye darts over the scene just as it darts arbitrarily over pictures, seemingly discovering what is there almost at random while the mind simultaneously fuses impressions into interpretations of experience.[16] The images of Calidore's vision still overlap and merge, but imitation of perception is not so obvious as in the passages where motion is involved.

We might say that the motion in the second major type of Scanning is lateral, whereas in the first it is frontal. In the second type, it is through or across, rather than straight toward, a scene or place. Therefore, this variety of Scanning is the broadest of all, encompassing not only scenes that might be represented in a panel picture, but vast accumulations of related scenes such as we might find in a fresco cycle, a huge mural, or a complex miniature painting that employs the continuous narrative method. Typically, the second type of Scanning is found in sustained passages which represent "places" such as the Bowre of Blisse or the Cave of Mammon. We must be careful, however, for "place" to us naturally implies "space"; but space in the poem tends to be created *ad hoc* for special purposes in restricted settings which are arranged against a neutral, spaceless ground. There are few empty pictorial spaces in *The Faerie Queene* into which figures move as they might move onto an empty stage with a perspective backdrop and wings. One example of such a space is Mount Acidale in Book Six (6.10.6-8), where a landscape appears as

[16] See Guy T. Buswell, *How People Look at Pictures* (Chicago, 1935).

an empty setting, until the approaching Calidore first hears and then sees the dancers.

A "place" in Faerie Land generally is not a continuous and integrated space to be Scanned, but a galaxy of highly localized scenes which stand in indeterminate, or at least tenuous, spatial relationships to each other, and together make up a setting. Spenser's representation of entire "places" in Faerie Land is governed by ordering principles similar to those in Framing. The places in *The Faerie Queene* tend to be set-pieces composed of medallions whose individual shapes are determined by what is represented within them. Moreover, the relationship of the discrete scenes to one another is more rhetorical than spatial, and the interstices of the galaxy of scenes that constitute a "place" are undefined and virtually blank. Particular visual experience is very important in them, but it is shaped into pictorial, iconographic, and descriptive forms which also carry a great burden of meaning. As an example of Spenser's procedure, the Cave of Mammon is particularly interesting because its organization marks and exaggerates Spenser's way of presenting experience. Since we have already considered the effect of context upon strictly nonpictorial materials, we can simplify the explanation of this episode by concentrating upon structure.

We do not get an immediate view of the cave into which Guyon follows Mammon, but learn that "the dore streight way/ Did shut, and from behind it forth there lept/ An vgly feend, more fowle then dismall day" (2.7.26). A stanza tells us of the fiend's intentions before this remarkable view of the first part of the cave is given:

> That houses forme within was rude and strong,
> Like an huge caue, hewne out of rocky clift,
> From whose rough vaut the ragged breaches hong,
> Embost with massy gold of glorious gift,

And with rich metall loaded euery rift,
That heauy ruine they did seeme to threat;
And ouer them *Arachne* high did lift
Her cunning web, and spred her subtile net,
Enwrapped in fowle smoke and clouds more blacke
    then Iet.

Both roofe, and floore, and wals were all of gold,
But ouergrowne with dust and old decay,
And hid in darkenesse, that none could behold
The hew thereof: for vew of chearefull day
Did neuer in that house it selfe display,
But a faint shadow of vncertain light;
Such as a lamp, whose life does fade away:
Or as the Moone cloathed with clowdy night,
Does shew to him, that walkes in feare and sad
    affright.

                      (2.7.28-29)

These stanzas overlap loosely with somewhat the effect of an inverted Focused image. The details in stanza twenty-eight are presented descriptively in a formulated order, and only with our discovery in the last line that the ceiling is "en-wrapped" in "clouds more blacke then Iet" does the former descriptive precision seem odd. The next stanza shows this surrealistic accuracy of detail to be a visual projection of the observer's terror, as revealed in the line, "That heauy ruine they did seeme to threat." The room's obscurity is modified only by a "faint shadow" of light which is exactly defined in a double reference to actual experiences of half-light.

By setting contradictory visual images together in these stanzas, Spenser reveals how closely intertwined are experi-ence of the visual world and fantasy metaphorically conceived as visual experience. He does not imply that one is more valid than the other, and ultimately they do not even seem contradictory. Both are attempts to give meaningful form to the present by referring it to the past, as Spenser shows when he echoes in stanza twenty-eight the description at Mammon's first appearance:

His yron coate all ouergrowne with rust,
Was vnderneath enueloped with gold,
Whose glistring glosse darkned with filthy dust,
Well it appeared, to haue beene of old
A worke of rich entayle, and curious mould,
Wouen with antickes and wild Imagery.

(2.7.4)

Mammon's embossed coat "darkned with filthy dust" appropriately provides the visual categories within which can be imagined the fearful details of a half-seen vault "Embost with massy gold of glorious gift." Beneath this vault there is "nothing to be seene" but an explicitly fearful collection of "yron chests and coffers strong" surrounded by "dead mens bones, which round about were flong." An intriguing space is created by these stanzas, full of faintly glimmering light, indistinct riches, and evidence of ignominious deaths. Yet nothing happens in it. It is an isolated image designed to show money as a fearful threat to human life; it governs our response to the debate which follows and comments upon every golden image that Mammon presents. Guyon and his tempter leave it immediately without comment and "forward passe, ne *Guyon* yet spoke word,/ Till that they came vnto an yron dore" (2.7.31).

The description of the room behind the door, which "shewd of richesse such exceeding store,/ As eye of man did neuer see before," is visually unspecific and the atmosphere of this tableau depends heavily upon the image of the preceding room. This room full of riches is not so much another space as an occasion for a debate between Mammon and Guyon. It

is interesting to speculate about the arrangement of this se-
quence: the store of riches could easily have been exposed
under the cave's encrusted main vault; but indistinct space
and "an yron dore" set the riches apart from that striking
first image. The debate about this hoard, which "Ne euer
could within one place be found" and therefore is probably
illusory, is carefully separated from the fearful vault as if these
images represented separate steps in a carefully constructed
argument whose progress through various topoi is expressed
by the icon of rooms whose relationship to each other is logical,
not spatial. The foyer of the House of Richesse is the visual
equivalent of an exordium.

And so the progress continues in the same pattern. Guyon
is "shortly brought/ Vnto another rowme" which proves to be
the smelting room, "the fountaine of the worldes good"—or
at least goods; then "through a darksome narrow strait,/ To
a broad gate, all built of beaten gold," within which stands
Disdayne. Each of these settings is the occasion for a separate
phase of Guyon's temptation. Disdayne's gate, separate and
striking in itself, is in function like the room full of riches or
the smelting room. It is like one of the mansions in a medieval
play, and also the entrance to Ambition's throne room which

> was large and wide,
> As it some Gyeld or solemne Temple weare:
> Many great golden pillours did vpbeare
> The massy roofe, and riches huge sustayne,
> And euery pillour decked was full deare
> With crownes and Diademes, and titles vaine,
> Which mortall Princes wore, whiles they on earth
> did rayne.
>
> (2.7.43)

Ambition herself, seen surrounded by "a route of people," is
presented in much the same way as Lucifera:

Her face right wondrous faire did seeme to bee,
That her broad beauties beam great brightnes threw
Through the dim shade, that all men might it see:
Yet was not that same her owne natiue hew,
But wrought by art and counterfetted shew,
Thereby more louers vnto her to call;
Nath'lesse most heauenly faire in deed and vew
She by creation was, till she did fall;
Thenceforth she sought for helps, to cloke her crime
    withall.

There, as in glistring glory she did sit,
She held a great gold chaine ylincked well,
Whose vpper end to highest heauen was knit,
And lower part did reach to lowest Hell;
And all that preace did round about her swell,
To catchen hold of that long chaine, thereby
To clime aloft, and others to excell:
That was *Ambition*, rash desire to sty,
And euery lincke thereof a step of dignity.

                             (2.7.45-46)

The rich architectural setting, the figure, the "great gold chaine" stretched between clouds at the top and "lowest Hell" (perhaps a hole with flames leaping out) at the bottom, the people trying to cling to the chain at different levels—this grouping is the figure for an emblem, and the epigrammatic last two lines of stanza forty-six are the motto or "Word" for it.

Guyon is "thence led/ Through griesly shadowes by a beaten path" into the Garden of Proserpina where, mansion-like, is found "in the midst thereof a siluer seat,/ With a thicke Arber goodly ouer dight." No space is represented, but

Next thereunto did grow a goodly tree,
With braunches broad dispred and body great,

Clothed with leaues, that none the wood mote see
And loaden all with fruit as thicke as it might bee.
(2.7.53)

Except for the next-to-last line, this is visually imprecise.
Spenser's diction is evasive in order to point his climactic ar-
rangement of tree, branches, leaves, and fruit culminating in
line one of stanza fifty-four, "Their fruit were golden apples
glistring bright." The two-stanza excursus which at first seems
to gloss these emblematic apples for us is a striking example
of Spenser's equivocal, or even enigmatic, encrustration of
myth.[17] Only after this mythographic digression does Spen-
ser present the garden as a place the compass of which is
defined by the gold-bearing tree, whose

> broad braunches, laden with rich fee,
> Did stretch themselues without the vtmost bound
> Of this great gardin, compast with a mound,
> Which ouer-hanging, they themselues did steepe,
> In a blacke flood which flow'd about it round;
> That is the riuer of *Cocytus* deepe,
> In which full many soules do endlesse waile and weepe.
> (2.7.56)

Here is a space sketched in outline where before there was
simply an arbor with a tree "next thereunto," but it remains
a sketch except where Spenser articulates the setting in which
Tantalus will shortly appear. This "great gardin" space figures

---

[17] See *The Poetry of The Faerie Queene*, pp. 244 and 271; and Frank
Kermode, "The Cave of Mammon" in *The Prince of Poets*, ed. John
R. Elliott, Jr. (New York and London, 1968), pp. 267-268. Spenser's
ambiguous use of mythology seems so far to have prevented critical
agreement concerning the meaning of this passage. The most recent
major study is Alpers', pp. 235-275, "Interpreting the Cave of Mam-
mon"; he discusses many different readings, especially Kermode's and
Harry Berger, Jr.'s, in *The Allegorical Temper* (New Haven, 1957),
"The Hero Faints: A Critical Misadventure," pp. 3-38.

forth an allegorical and psychological relationship among the silver seat, the golden apples, and the river. It represents a transition in the argument, which continues on its perimeter as Guyon meets Tantalus and Pilate. Only in stanza sixty-three, when Mammon desperately directs Guyon's attention away from Pilate, do his demonstratives increase our sense of spatial continuity: "Why takest not of that same fruit of gold,/ Ne sittest downe on that same siluer stoole." Having resisted the temptations of the Underworld and having at last seen its most pitiful and unglamorous occupants, Guyon resists Mammon's invitation "to rest thy wearie person, in the shadow coole," asks to depart, and once outside is plunged into the darkness of a faint.

In this brief account of the Cave of Mammon, I have purposely emphasized the transitions from one part of the cave to the next. No matter how vivid each scene may be in itself—whether it contains its own internal action, is an Emblem like Ambition, or like the room full of riches has no particular visual content (the effect would collapse if there were many of these)—the connections between individual scenes are spatially indeterminate. The Cave of Mammon is the sum of these scenes, but as a whole it is not spatially conceived. Neither is it governed by time, for Guyon's passage of three days in the cave is not mentioned until he faints.

Because it is a cave, the spatial arrangement of Mammon's realm is superficially plausible, but like many other "places" in *The Faerie Queene* it is a cluster of isolated pictorial images, icons, and descriptions. Recently, Frances A. Yates in her pioneering study *The Art of Memory* has described a medieval and Renaissance tradition which may help to explain the spatial peculiarities of the Cave of Mammon, and perhaps of other Spenserian set-pieces as well.[18] The architectural settings

[18] (Chicago and London, 1966). Spenser's traditional representation

in the cave, which modern readers accept so readily as attempted literal representations of physical space, may really be mental spaces architecturally conceived. I have already shown that Spenser alerts us to this possibility in the two stanzas that seem to represent the House of Richesse (2.7.28-29), and that the relationship of places in the cave is more argumentative than spatial. The things that Mammon shows Guyon appear to be *imagines agentes*, as they are called in the memory tradition—"remarkably beautiful, crowned, richly dressed, or remarkably hideous and grotesque."[19] Placed in architecturally designed settings so that we can recall their proper order, they each figure forth an argumentative point about Mammon's realm and they each contain the *intentio* that we should avoid the unnatural moral or spiritual state they so vividly represent.[20] According to Bacon in the *Advancement of Learning*, the two purposes of the art of memory are to order our understandings of things and to make them into striking emblems so that our "practique" may be improved; to him there is definite moral usefulness in well-arranged memory images.[21] In other works he describes how the two traditional parts of the art of memory accomplish these purposes: first, memory places "may be either Places in the proper sense of the word, as a door, a corner, a window, and the like; or familiar and well known persons; or anything we choose (provided they are arranged in a certain order)"; second, "Emblems bring down intellectual to sensible things; for what is sensible always strikes the memory

---

of the mind as an emblem of Prudence, of which memory is a part, is well known (2.9.47ff.).

[19] *The Art of Memory*, p. 92.

[20] On the term *"intentio"* see *The Art of Memory*, p. 64.

[21] *Advancement of Learning*, 2.15.2; in *Works*, ed. James Spedding, R. L. Ellis, and D. D. Heath (New York, 1869-1870), III, 398-399; quoted by Yates, p. 371.

stronger, and sooner impresses itself than the intellectual."[22] Spenser's linear, argumentative ordering of images in the Cave of Mammon's architecturally conceived space is almost certainly dependent upon the traditional art of memory.

Most of the pictorial imagery we have analyzed thus far, with the exception of a few larger sequences, has been limited to the mimesis of extremely particular visual phenomena, either in isolation or as the vivifying elements in wider contexts containing some descriptive materials. Paradoxically, when the same poetic techniques of fragmentation and shattering are sustained and applied in the set-pieces to a number of closely related scenes and figures, the result is frequently pictorial but rarely evokes a consistent or illusionistic space. Spenser's technique of lateral Scanning encourages us to perceive space not as a continuum but as a series of individual subjective experiences. But pictorial vividness and the illusionism of consistent spatial construction should be equated no more in poetry than in the visual arts, where selective realism is a recognized phase in the history of representation. As John White observes in *The Birth and Rebirth of Pictorial Space*, "it is generally agreed that both in primitive art and in the reviving naturalism of the period leading up to the Renaissance an interest in the object itself precedes any interest in space as such. The interval, or nothingness, which separates one solid from the next, is relatively unimportant."[23] Immediate and complicated response to individual visual phenomena in works of art need not be irrevocably linked to the presentation of space in the simultaneous, geometric totality of linear perspective. Although a perspective context can enhance the impact of closely observed detail, a most cursory study of the visual arts in the late Middle Ages and early Renaissance will

[22] *Novum Organum*, 2.26, *Works*, 1, 275; and *De Augmentis Scientiarum*, 5.5, *Works*, 1, 649. Both quoted by Yates, p. 371.
[23] (London, 1957), p. 35.

reveal that individual objects often are rendered in precise "realistic" detail in wholly incongruous contexts, even quite out of scale with their surroundings.

As we have several times observed, Spenser's continuing encounter with the individual phenomena of visual experience, his self-conscious use of literary forms, and his historical sensibility are all markedly post-medieval. But his treatment of space in *The Faerie Queene* may justifiably be called Gothic— or more properly, Neo-Gothic. Joseph B. Dallett's discussion of the tapestries in Spenser's poem has anticipated and influenced my application of this term. We are mutually dependent upon Dagobert Frey's distinction between Gothic and Renaissance modes of representation, accurately summarized by Dallett, as a contrast "between space presented to the fixed eye of the observer as a simultaneous, geometric totality, a medium receding with the speed of light into distant perspective and demarcated by a uniform scale for the figures and objects in it, and space presented only as a constant alteration or movement in the subjective experience of the observer as he views the elements of the work successively, in time."[24] Linear perspective presents a space in which the relationships

[24] "Ideas of Sight in *The Faerie Queene*," *ELH*, xxvii (1960), 99-100 and n. 29. The title of Frey's work is *Gotik und Renaissance als Grundlagen der modernen Weltanschauung* (Augsburg, 1929). See also Wilhelm Worringer, *Form in Gothic*, ed. Herbert Read (London, 1927); Emile Mâle, *The Gothic Image*, trans. Dora Nussey (New York, 1958); and D. W. Robertson, Jr., *A Preface to Chaucer* (Princeton, 1962), pp. 138-285, "Late Medieval Style," for an extensive illustrated comparison between art and literature in the Middle Ages, especially in Chaucer's period. Dallett's analysis of techniques in *The Faerie Queene* which are analogous to the continuous narrative method in the visual arts, particularly in Gothic, is grounded upon a firm awareness of methodological difficulties (p. 98). Dallett's analogies with the fine arts are supported by a careful literary study of the way things are seen within the poem; he is, as Alpers says, an extreme exponent of the view that descriptions in the poem are intended to represent "real" objects. See *The Poetry of The Faerie Queene*, p. 9, n. 5.

of objects to one another can be studied by an eye which is fixed by a convention of art. It is "an approximation to an infinite, mathematically homogeneous space, and the creation of a new, and powerful means of giving unity to the pictorial design."[25] Part of the illusion that Renaissance paintings create when viewed under proper conditions is the illusion of simultaneity which, given an acceptance of the proper conventions, poetry also is able to achieve. Such simultaneous relationships are not rendered by the discontinuous and fragmented anatomizing which is characteristic of the Gothic in art—and of *The Faerie Queene*. Presumably the reiterated imagery of Focusing, the suspended effects of Framing, or even the first type of Scanning could be used to create still more continuous pictorial spaces like the scene of Mount Acidale. Spenser must have known something of Renaissance representations of continuous perspective space, even though he appears to have taken discontinuous forms to be normal visual renderings. In detail Spenser's pictures are works of the Renaissance, but his large-scale effects, though they too include vivid detail, are very different.

What is the explanation for Spenser's Neo-Gothic treatment of space? There are several possible answers to this question. It is well-known that the Renaissance in the North, especially in England, did not develop as smoothly and straightforwardly

[25] *The Birth and Rebirth of Pictorial Space*, p. 124. "The artificial perspective which Alberti codified and himself conceived in part, and which dominated Italian art throughout the fifteenth century, has four principal characteristics. . . . (a) There is no distortion of straight lines. (b) There is no distortion, or foreshortening, of objects or distances parallel to the picture plane, which is therefore given a particular emphasis. (c) Orthogonals converge to a single vanishing point dependent on the fixed position of the observer's eye. (d) The size of objects diminishes in an exact proportion to their distance from this observer, so that all quantities are measurable" (123-124). See also James J. Gibson, "Pictures, Perspective, and Perception," *Daedalus*, LXXXIX (1960), 216-227.

as in Italy. In the North, strange mixtures of old and new may be found at surprisingly late dates; thus, we probably should not be shocked to discover that Spenser's disposition of space is structurally similar to Chaucer's, although new perceptual schemes are beginning to appear in the Renaissance work. Moreover, particularly during the 1570's and 1580's, there was a considerable vogue of Neo-Medievalism at Elizabeth's court, where the world of Arthurian legend and of the Romances was translated into dynastic propaganda and into ritual. Courtiers tilted in knightly garb before a Queen who delighted in stately Progresses to visit great archaic castles built as settings for her own glorification as a cult figure. In painting, apparently by the Queen's own choice, the decorative, self-conscious archaism of Nicholas Hilliard's portraits replaced the realistic "shadowed" style of Flanders that had appeared in English portraiture during the previous generation.[26] Spenser writes in the midst of a sophisticated revival

[26] See Roy C. Strong, "Elizabethan Neo-Medievalism," pp. 13-21 in *The English Icon* (London and New York, 1969): "The sun-lit world of medieval manuscript illumination with its ultramarines, pinks and yellows and its lavish use of real gold and silver is the visual vocabulary deployed by the exponents of the Hilliardesque" (p. 15). On the revival of the dying conventions of chivalry at court and their connections with the vogue for Romances see the discussion and citations in *Allegorical Imagery*, Chapter Five, especially pp. 340-342 and 388-389. Another possible explanation for this revival, interesting but admittedly difficult to document, is that Spenser is no less conscious of his archaic treatment of space than he is of his archaic language, and that his medievalizing is part of a fashion observable in Continental Mannerist art and art criticism. On the affinities of Mannerist art and art theory with medieval art and philosophy see Otto Benesch, *The Art of the Renaissance in Northern Europe* (Cambridge, Mass., 1945), pp. 35, 91, 120, 124, *et passim*; Sir Anthony Blunt, *Artistic Theory in Italy, 1450-1600* (Oxford, 1962), especially pp. 137-159, "The Later Mannerists." See also John Pope-Hennessy, "Nicholas Hilliard and Mannerist Art Theory," *JWCI*, VI (1943), 89-100; and Roy C. Strong, *Portraits of Queen Elizabeth I* (Oxford, 1963), pp. 33-41. Admittedly the high Renaissance style—especially of Raphael—that

of a medieval past whose ceremonies had, in any event, survived remarkably well and for which his own imaginative sympathy was extraordinary. He represents his antique world in a mode that was at once slightly out-dated and enormously fashionable. His devotion to medieval forms was certainly not frivolous, but it was very much of its time. His active encounter with visual phenomena, as opposed to exclusive reliance on schemata, marks him as a post-medieval artist, yet his discontinuous treatment of space may appropriately be called Gothic.

Mannerism assumes and partly reacts against never existed in England, but *forms* can be adopted without their original resonances.

CHAPTER FIVE

Pictorial Vision in the
Poetry of Spenser

S penser's development as a pictorial poet does not fall
into a pattern which can be traced in the minor poems
or in *The Faerie Queene*, nor is his pictorialism a con-
sistent feature of an early, middle, or late "style." The few
instances of full-blown pictorial imagery in the minor poems
are fairly late, but some late works—the *Amoretti*, for exam-
ple—seem notably unpictorial by comparison with such others
as the *Epithalamion* and the *Prothalamion*. I have taken *The
Faerie Queene* as the preeminent example of Spenser's pic-
torialism, but we do not have enough definitive chronological
evidence about the poem's composition to trace the develop-
ment of his use of pictorial techniques.[1] However, it may still
prove useful to survey Spenser's works from the special point
of view defined in the previous chapters, by looking first at
some of the minor poems and then by studying the imagery
of the most brilliant and sustained compendium of pictorial-
ism in *The Faerie Queene*, the Bowre of Blisse.

The Earlier Poems: Emblems and Icons

Spenser's earliest known work was published in 1569, and
is generally known by its running title, *A Theatre for World-
lings*. It contains translations of poems by Petrarch and Du-
Bellay, woodcuts illustrating the poems, and a long prose ex-
position. There are many theories about Spenser's contribu-

---

[1] On the composition of the poem see Josephine Waters Bennett,
The Evolution of "The Faerie Queene" (Chicago, 1942) and W.J.B.
Owen, "The Structure of *The Faerie Queene*," *PMLA*, LXVIII (1953),
1079-1100.

tion to the volume, but it is agreed that the translations are largely his: Spenser himself as much as claimed them at a time late in his career when he was hardly likely to publish as his own the minor efforts of another poet.[2] It has been called the first emblem book produced in England, but first or not, it meets most of the basic requirements of the genre, and raises issues central to the consideration of Spenser's pictorialism.[3]

Emblem writing as conceived by Alciati and as generally

[2] In his *Complaints* (1591) the poems by Petrarch were included after slight revisions under the heading "formerly translated," and the poems by DuBellay were changed from blank verse into rhymed sonnets. For information about the work see *Variorum*, 8.273-280, 409-416, and 624-627. See also Harold Stein, *Studies in Spenser's Complaints* (New York, 1934), pp. 67-70 and 107-151; Alfred W. Satterthwaite, *Spenser, Ronsard, and DuBellay* (Princeton, 1960), pp. 25-36 and 255-263; Francis R. Johnson, *A Critical Bibliography of the Works of Edmund Spenser Printed Before 1700* (London, 1933); Arthur M. Hind, *Engraving in England in the Sixteenth and Seventeenth Centuries*, I, "The Tudor Period" (Cambridge, 1952). Additionally, for brief comments, Rosemary Freeman, *English Emblem Books* (London, 1948), pp. 51-52 and 101-102; Samuel C. Chew, *The Pilgrimage of Life* (New Haven, 1962), p. 285. Hind, pp. 122-123, says that the woodcuts are copied from 1568 Dutch and French editions of the *Theatre* in which etchings by Marcus Gheeraerts the Elder appeared. The woodcuts are crude by comparison with the etchings and most of them are mirror images of the originals (graphic copies of other works of art are often reversed, for obvious reasons), but six are not. Facsimiles of the poems and woodcuts are printed in *Variorum*, 8. 3-25. Hind, Pl. 50, reproduces four of Gheeraerts's original etchings.

[3] Freeman, p. 51, all but agrees, and cites C. H. Herford, *Literary Relations between England and Germany in the Sixteenth Century* (London, 1886), p. 369 and Harold Stein, p. 111. To these I can add Chew, p. 285. The book's method of composition was very close to Alciati's as Mario Praz describes it: "Alciati, in addition to hieroglyphics, utilized the epigrams of the *Greek Anthology*. In many cases he translated single Greek epigrams into Latin and added the figure which was called for by the text." *Encyclopedia of World Art*, IV, 728.

practiced in the Renaissance was essentially literary in char-
acter even though the illustrations were theoretically impor-
tant. Elaborate Renaissance theorizing which asserts the rela-
tionship between figure and motto in emblems to be like
that between body and soul automatically assigns a priority
which perhaps indicates more about the function of emblem
pictures than this illustrative metaphor was designed to re-
veal: the soul exists independently of the body, which can
easily be cast off and whose beauty is irrelevant.[4] Any interest
the picture as an aesthetic object may have for the emblematist
is ancillary to its primary function as a sign. The different
sets of illustrations for *A Theatre for Worldlings* demonstrate
this point amply. The etchings found in the Continental edi-
tions are not masterpieces, but there is a certain fineness and
delicacy to them. On the other hand, the woodcut copies used
in the English edition are crude: they gloss over fine distant
landscapes and genre detail, and despite approximate perspec-
tive copied from the originals they render the subject in the
flat form of an icon. Still, the woodcuts serve their purpose,
for the emblematist is interested not so much in pictures *qua*
pictures as in their ability to function as iconographic signs.
The end of his pictorial and conceptual signs is the same, but
their means appeal to different senses: as Henry Peacham says
of the emblem, "the true vse heereof from time to time onely
hath beene, *Vtile dulci miscere*, to feede at once both the

---

[4] The comparison is a commonplace in writings on emblems and
imprese. See for example the commentary on Alciati by Claudius
Minos, *Emblemata* (Antwerp, 1577), p. 20; also Freeman, pp. 39-42
and Jean H. Hagstrum, *The Sister Arts* (Chicago and London, 1958),
pp. 94-96.
    [5] Quoted by Hagstrum, *The Sister Arts*, p. 96, n. 12. The theory of
visual signs is an important topic in Renaissance philosophy and
criticism; see E. H. Gombrich, "Icones Symbolicae: The Visual Image
in Neo-Platonic Thought," *JWCI*, xi (1948), 163-192.

minde, and eie. . . ."[5] No matter how much the reader's eye may be delighted he must still confront the emblem's enigma intellectually. Since the iconographic elements of almost any emblem can be named, listed, or described without reference to their formal organization or pictorial impression, there can be no sharp distinction between emblem books as such and emblems found in the tradition of iconic or emblematic poetry. As Hagstrum has observed, the poem can create and carry within itself its own visual referents. The epigram, for example, is often ecphrastic despite its separation from the sculpture on which it was inscribed either in reality or in the imagination; an emblematic poem "verbally creates or implies its own design. The title of the poem or the metaphorical words of its text may bring an image to mind, which then becomes the emblem of the poem, the 'visual' embodiment of its abstract meaning."[6]

Emblematic poems of the kind Spenser translated for the *Theatre* were, in effect, modern epigrams waiting for an Alciati to add figures to them, but the figures in the volume are not so much complements as echoes of the poems. Most are organized by antitheses; the speaker describes a remarkable or beautiful thing, then sees it fallen, killed, or destroyed. Half of the figures are similarly organized, and represent two opposed states of the subject continuously narrated in a single setting ("Epigrams," 1-6; "Sonets," 2-6). In other cases the figure simply represents the before or the after ("Epigrams," 4; "Sonets," 7, 9, and 10). The rest of the poems describe one unchanging sight, and the figures attempt to represent it ("Sonets," 8 and 11; "Visions of Revelation," 1-4).

[6] *The Sister Arts*, p. 98. This quotation refers to seventeenth-century poetry, but can reasonably be extended to earlier periods. Mario Praz, *Studies in Seventeenth-Century Imagery*, 2nd ed. (Rome, 1964), pp. 22-23, says that "many epigrams in the *Greek Anthology* written for statues are emblems in all but name."

The figures add little to one's understanding of the emblem contained in each poem, but many of the limitations of *A Theatre for Worldlings* are inherent in the genre. One cannot deny that editions of the *Theatre* containing the etchings at least approach the goal of *utile dulci miscere*, but the high-flown theoretical goal of perfect mutual dependence of figure and word cannot be realized through pictorial subtlety. The peculiar aesthetic satisfaction emblems are supposed to bring arises not so much from the skillful creation of an image as from the skillful alliance of the image's meaning with the meaning of the words accompanying it. The *Theatre* deserves emphasis because it marks the direction Spenser would take, for much of his subsequent writing, including many things in *The Faerie Queene*, is firmly rooted in the tradition of iconic and ecphrastic poetry.[7] Emblem books must be understood as part of these predominantly literary traditions, not

[7] See Chapter Two, note 23 for my definitions of these terms and a comment on Hagstrum's. See also *The Sister Arts*, p. 18, n. 34. Renaissance works that are iconic or emblematic in character are perhaps, as Hagstrum says, best understood as "related to the iconic [ecphrastic] tradition in poetry, to the ideals of the critics, to antecedent poetic pictorialism—to the type of visual effect that derives from these areas of predominantly literary concern" (p. 78). Nonetheless, I do not feel that all Renaissance pictorialism is founded in this tradition; Hagstrum places Spenser squarely in this tradition, and singles out one poem, *Amoretti*, LXVII, as "pictorial." Hagstrum says that in this poem Spenser's "whole manner of seeing and of proceeding is pictorial rather than directly iconic [ecphrastic]. Though no tapestry or painting is in view, the scene is plastically conceived; and the concluding couplet is like nothing so much as the kind of epigram that in antiquity was placed under a statue, a painting, or an urn" (p. 80). "Emblematic" is perhaps a better term to apply to the poem, especially since its structure is similar to the poems in *A Theatre for Worldlings*, the difference being that most of them represent an action in two parts whereas this poem has three. A continuously narrated woodcut or etching could still represent the poem's major elements, even though the literary nuances would be lost. The *Amoretti* are remarkably short of pictorial imagery as I have defined it.

as sources of influence from the visual arts.[8] The bulk of the so-called pictorialism of the minor poems is best termed iconic, emblematic, or descriptive rather than pictorial: not only the obvious cases of the *Theatre* and the later *Visions* based on it but much in *The Shepheardes Calender, The Ruines of Time, Virgil's Gnat, Muiopotmos*, and the *Amoretti*. In my discussion of Scanning I have already shown quasi-pictorial materials to be elements of the pervasive pictorialism of *The Faerie Queene*. However, pictorial techniques are not so prominent in the minor poems, so most of the iconic, emblematic, and descriptive content of these works remains inert by comparison with *The Faerie Queene*, which is pictorially energized.

The Shepheardes Calender (1579) is the second and last of Spenser's illustrated works.[9] The woodcuts in it are as elementary in execution as those in *A Theatre for Worldlings*, and far less closely related to the poems they illustrate. Six of them do show something from the events of the poem, but the others contribute no more than an appropriate number of shepherds debating, singing, or playing.[10] In a postscript to one of his letters to Harvey, Spenser seems to hint that their purpose may have been to make the book more salable by filling it out and making it look something like an emblem book: "I take best my *Dreames* shoulde come forth alone, being growen by meanes of the Glosse . . . full as great as my *Calendar*. Therin be some things excellently, and many things wittily discoursed of *E. K.* and the Pictures so singu-

---

[8] For examples of such attributions of influence see "Emblems and the 'Visions,' " *Variorum*, 8.624-627, especially the quotation from Friedland. Also, Henry Green, *Shakespeare and the Emblem Writers* (London, 1870).

[9] The first volume of *The Faerie Queene* contains a single woodcut of St. George.

[10] In the first group are *January, February, March, April, May,* and *November*; in the second, *June, July, August, September, October,* and *December*.

larly set forth, and purtrayed, as if *Michael Angelo* were there, he could (I think) nor amende the best, nor reprehende the worst."[11] In view of Spenser's association with Leicester, who had a great art collection, with the court, and apparently with a number of collectors of medieval illuminated manuscripts at Cambridge, one would like, as the *Variorum* editor says, "to believe that this passage is not *extra iocum*."[12]

Rosemary Freeman is certainly right when she says that "apart from the use of mottoes, *The Shepheardes Calender* is not particularly emblematic except when fables are introduced."[13] The mottoes appear at the end of each poem (they are called "Emblemes" in the text and E. K. calls them "Emblemes" or "Poesyes" in his Glosse for "Januarye"); the two fables in the *Calender* have additional epigrammatic mottoes, morals, or tags at the end. In "Febrvarie" Thenot says, "Such was thend of this ambitious brere,/ For scorning Eld" (237-238), and in "Maye" Piers concludes with "Such end had the Kidde, for he nould warned be/ Of craft, coloured with simplicitie" (302-303). There is perhaps an emblematic touch in "March" when Thomalin tells of Cupid's appearance to him:

> With that sprong forth a naked swayne,
> With spotted winges like Peacocks trayne,
>   And laughing lope to a tree.
> His gylden quiuer at his backe,
> And siluer bowe, which was but slacke,
>   Which lightly he bent at me.   (79-84)

One of the "Emblemes" at the end would do well as a motto—
"*To be wise and eke to loue,/ Is graunted scarce to God aboue.*" There are other emblems, but visual materials are

---

[11] *Variorum*, 9.18.

[12] *Variorum*, 9.268. See Chapter One, note 30 on Spenser's exposure to the fine arts.

[13] *English Emblem Books*, p. 102.

sparingly used in *The Shepheardes Calender* and pictorial techniques are almost completely absent.

One of the chief reasons for the *Calender*'s visual plainness is the apparent uncongeniality of the poetry of debate with the inherently illogical expansiveness, the *copia*, of pictorial imagery. One can see the importance of plenitude to an increase of energy in even tiny visual effects, as well as Spenser's natural tendency toward elaborately concentrated imagery, by observing his treatment of a detail in the figure of Verlame near the beginning of *The Ruines of Time*:

> There on the other side, I did behold
> A Woman sitting sorrowfullie wailing,
> Rending her yeolow locks, like wyrie golde,
> About her shoulders careleslie downe trailing,
> And streames of teares from her faire eyes forth
>   railing.[14]

This description is based upon the figure of Rome in a poem by DuBellay which also appears, as translated by Spenser, in the volume of *Complaints*:

> Hard by a riuers side a virgin faire,
> Folding her armes to heauen with thousand throbs,
> And outraging her cheekes and golden haire,
> To falling riuers sound thus tun'd her sobs.[15]

In *The Ruines of Time* Spenser has changed DuBellay's

[14] Lines 8-12. The date of *The Ruines of Time* is hotly debated, but this part is generally thought to be early. See *Complaints*, ed. W. L. Renwick (London, 1928), p. 190; *Studies in Spenser's Complaints*, pp. 40-41; and *Variorum*, 8.526-530.

[15] The original poem from the *Songe* of DuBellay is quoted in *Variorum*, 8.285:

> Sur la rive d'un fleuve une Nymphe esploree,
> Croisant les bras au ciel avec mille sanglotz,
> Accordoit ceste plainte au murmure des flotz,
> Oultrageant son beau teinct, & sa tresse doree.

frantic nymph into a woman who concentrates upon a single action; our attention is fixed to the "yeolow locks," and the epithets devoted to her golden hair are syntactically isolated by enclosing participles. "Like wyrie golde," is balanced between "rending" and "trailing," so that lines ten and eleven become a closed system with its own internal balance. This discrete cluster of visual details is similar, on a small scale, to formally isolated Focused and Framed images. In *The Ruines of Time* Spenser eliminates a dramatic gesture, working instead for stasis and a concentrated visual effect. There is usually just such an elimination of gesture in his imitations of Ariosto and Tasso. His earliest version of the DuBellay in *A Theatre for Worldlings* provides a sharp contrast:

> Hard by a riuers side, a wailing Nimphe,
> Folding hir armes with thousand sighs to heauen
> Did tune hir plaint to falling riuers sound,
> Renting hir faire visage and golden haire.
>
> ("Sonets," 8)

We rush from one action to the next, and the visual references are scattered; Spenser's revision in the *Complaints* is more orderly, but only in *The Ruines of Time* does he put a single action before us with the plenitude and exactness to give the image almost pictorial force.

In *The Shepheardes Calender* visual materials remain for the most part static and unenlarged; the one exception is Colin's "laye/ Of fayre *Elisa*" in the "Aprill" eclogue. After an exordium, as E. K. calls it, and a stanza rather strangely tracing Elisa's parentage to Syrinx and Pan, the poet calls our attention to her appearance:

> See, where she sits vpon the grassie greene,
>   (O seemely sight)
> Yclad in Scarlot like a mayden Queene,
>   And Ermines white.

Vpon her head a Cremosin coronet,
With Damaske roses and Daffadillies set:
  Bayleaues betweene,
  And Primroses greene
Embellish the sweete Violet.

Tell me, haue ye seene her angelick face,
  Like *Phoebe* fayre?
Her heauenly haueour, her princely grace
  can you well compare?
The Redde rose medled with the White yfere,
In either cheeke depeincten liuely chere.
  Her modest eye,
    Her Maiestie,
Where haue you seene the like, but there?

I sawe *Phoebus* thrust out his golden hedde,
  vpon her to gaze:
But when he sawe, how broade her beames did
  spredde, it did him amaze.
He blusht to see another Sunne belowe,
Ne durst againe his fyrye face out showe.

(55-78)

This passage shows that pictorial effects depend significantly upon the presence of rhetorical occasions appropriate to *copia*. Unless images become, in effect, the subject of debate or argument as they do in the Cave of Mammon episode, there will generally be no room for them in argumentative poetry. It is not surprising, then, that the comparative leisure of a complimentary lyric is the occasion for the closest approach to pictorial imagery in *The Shepheardes Calender*.

The pastoral image of Elisa is best understood as a heavenly parallel to the infernal image of Lucifera; this queen is enthroned not in gold but on a green, decorated not with jewels but with flowers, and compared to her own advantage with

Phoebus himself. There is, at the beginning, something of the accumulation of comparisons important to Focusing, but the crown is composed more of names than of things seen. The shift from Elisa's crown to her face is reminiscent of the breaking and shifting in Scanning, but "Her heauenly haueour, her princely grace" and "Her modest eye,/ Her Maiestie" are rather abstract. The descriptive metaphors are entirely conventional, including the hyperbolic turn to myth in order to explain Elisa's beauty by comparing it with the sun. There is a loose climactic sequence, as the poet enlarges upon his subject; the effect might be called pictorial except for its diffuseness and simple, iconic metaphors. It is at least interesting as an example of Spenser's approach to pictorialism fairly early in his career.

Later, in *Colin Clouts Come Home Againe*, which presumably was written after Spenser's trip to England in 1589-1590, he resorts to a more copious iconic emblem of "*Cynthiaes* presence" in order to show Elizabeth without mentioning her face:

> Such greatnes I cannot compare to ought:
> But if I her like ought on earth might read,
> I would her lyken to a crowne of lillies,
> Vpon a virgin brydes adorned head,
> With Roses dight and Goolds and Daffadillies;
> Or like the circlet of a Turtle true,
> In which all colours of the rainbow bee;
> Or like faire *Phebes* garlond shining new,
> In which all pure perfection one may see.
>
> (335-343)

The poet's role as mediator, so frequently felt in *The Faerie Queene*, is entirely explicit in this description. We begin with a slight variation on the familiar floral crown, but here instead of an ornament to the Queen's outward beauty, it is a symbol which manifests her being to the coarse human eye and understanding. Routine hyperbole is inadequate, so Spenser adds the iridescent band from the Turtledove's neck and finally the halo or rainbow that surrounds the moon. Progression from the first reference in this compound image to the last two seems strained because of Spenser's attempt to attach appropriate iconographic significance to the pastoral garland by connecting it with the rainbow and the moon-rainbow, as well as incidentally with the dove. The association of Elizabeth with the moon requires no gloss, but the significance of this elaborate icon's other components is clarified by the "Rainbow" portrait of Elizabeth at Hatfield House (Frontispiece). In this picture the Queen, who appears young despite the date of about 1600, is richly dressed in a costume ornamented with symbols of Fame, *Intelligenza*, and *Consiglio*; a jewelled crescent with pearls surmounts her headdress and she holds a rainbow above which is inscribed "Non Sine Sole Iris." Like the portrait, Spenser's icon ignores the fact of Elizabeth's age.[16] Spenser combines the dove and the rainbow, another traditional symbol of peace; then, in a brilliant stroke of synthesis, he fuses the sun's rainbow with the moon's and revitalizes two of the most conventional conceits for flattering the Queen. This densely contrived synthesis depends upon visual observation but Spenser's presentation is basically emblematic and iconic. His purpose is not to reveal Elizabeth's personality or to depict her actual appearance at a certain age, but, as in *The Faerie Queene*, to show "the

[16] For a description of the portrait's iconography see Roy C. Strong, *Portraits of Queen Elizabeth I* (Oxford, 1963), pp. 85-86. Like this one, a number of the later portraits of Elizabeth employ what Strong calls the "Hilliard Mask of Youth"; see p. 9 and plates xviii-xix. One of the very few portraits to show Elizabeth as an old woman is the "Ditchley" portrait now in the National Portrait Gallery (Strong, plate XV). After the Armada, portraits of the Queen printed on single leaves were evidently sold as "cult images"; see Strong, p. 31.

most high, mightie and magnificent Empresse renowmed for pietie, vertue, and all gratious government" (Dedication).

Better known than the icon in *Colin Clout* is the heraldic image of Elizabeth as Mercilla in Book Five of *The Faerie Queene*. Again, the aging Queen's face is not explicitly represented, and as one critic has said, "the visual details mark spiritual not actual realities."[17] I quote only those central lines which represent her canopy of state as a metaphorical cloud which clothes her dazzling brightness:

> All ouer her a cloth of state was spred,
> Not of rich tissew, nor of cloth of gold,
> Nor of ought else, that may be richest red,
> But like a cloud, as likest may be told,
> That her brode spreading wings did wyde vnfold;
> Whose skirts were bordred with bright sunny beams,
> Glistring like gold, amongst the plights enrold,
> And here and there shooting forth siluer streames,
> Mongst which crept litle Angels through the
>   glittering gleames.
>
> Seemed those litle Angels did vphold
> The cloth of state, and on their purpled wings
> Did beare the pendants, through their nimblesse bold.
>
>   (5.9.28-29)

A few stanzas later the Queen is specifically likened to the sun (5.9.35). In stanza twenty-eight the cloud-canopy shot through with beams of sunlight momentarily becomes a richly pleated princely garment such as Elizabeth wore at court. The pun on "pendants," a technical term in both the dress and the architecture of the time, lightly continues this conceit, which, outside of its heraldic context, seems stylized almost to the

---

[17] Jane Aptekar, *Icons of Justice: Iconography and Thematic Imagery in Book V of The Faerie Queene* (New York and London, 1969), p. 13; see pp. 13-17 and 70-76, *et passim*.

point of absurdity.[18] The purpose is celebration, not depiction. These icons of Elizabeth show that copious visual detail is an occasion for Spenser's pictorialism, not its cause, and that his disparate ways of seeing are difficult to harmonize. Often in the minor poems, as in the icon from *Colin Clout*, Spenser shows exact powers of observation, but the iconic imagery which he employs for explicitly allegorical purposes dominates less obtrusively symbolic visual images.

Pictorialism in the Minor Poems

Three of Spenser's minor poems, all later works, deserve special attention because of the sustained and striking detail of their visual references; I doubt that any attentive reader of Spenser would fail to name them—the *Muiopotmos*, the *Epithalamion*, and the *Prothalamion*.[19] In addition to an almost continuous flow of descriptive, iconic, and emblematic materials, each of these poems also contains one of the three examples of Focusing in the minor poems.

The *Muiopotmos*, one of Spenser's most extended pieces of ecphrastic writing, is laden with visual references. The arming of the butterfly Clarion near the beginning of the epillyon ends with a picture of his wings which is the controlling or energizing image of this work. The stanzas preceding the image of Clarion's wings liken the parts of the butterfly to parts of a suit of armor: "His breastplate first, that was of

18 *OED*, "Plight," 1.1; "Plait," 1.a; and "Pendant," 11.2.b and 11.5.a.
19 The *Epithalamion* and *Prothalamion* are among Spenser's last works; see *Variorum*, 8.645-652 and 662-666. *Muiopotmos*, which appears in *Complaints* (1591) with a separate title page dated 1590, is widely agreed to have been written shortly before publication. See *Studies in Spenser's Complaints*, pp. 65-66 and *Variorum*, 8.598-599. The allegory of the poem is problematic. See *Variorum*, 8.599-608; Don Cameron Allen, "Muiopotmos, or The Fate of the Butterflie," in *Image and Meaning* (Baltimore, 1960), pp. 20-41; and Hallett Smith, "The Use of Conventions in Spenser's Minor Poems," *Form and Convention in the Poetry of Edmund Spenser*, ed. William Nelson (New York and London, 1961), pp. 122-145.

substance pure," and about his shoulders "An hairie hide of some wilde beast," while he wore "Vpon his head his glistering Burganet," and "Therein two deadly weapons fixt he bore" (57, 66, 73, and 81). As a description, the comparison in series of these attributes with similar mythological objects remains fairly abstract, but the parts of the butterfly do come to the mind's eye. The climactic image of Clarion's wings seems odd in the armorial context, but the light bathos of this incongruity is appropriate to Spenser's mock-epic tone and is even heightened by the pictorial presentation:

> Lastly his shinie wings as siluer bright,
> Painted with thousand colours, passing farre
> All Painters skill, he did about him dight:
> Not halfe so manie sundrie colours arre
> In *Iris* bowe, ne heauen doth shine so bright,
> Distinguished with manie a twinckling starre,
> Nor *Iunoes* Bird in her ey-spotted traine
> So manie goodly colours doth containe.
>
> (89-96)

The components of this Focused image are negative comparisons which move rapidly from the general to the particular and from the familiar to the exotic; they are synthesized only momentarily in the strange luminescence of peacock feathers. The wings are like "siluer bright" and colorfully painted beyond anything man can make. They are also richer than the rainbow, brighter than the heavens, and more variegated than the tail of the heavenly bird itself. Formal arrangement and perceptual sequence coincide exactly in this stanza. The comparisons begin with the wings' brightness, then move to their color, return to their brilliance, and finally combine both in one image. But the acuity of our apprehension increases with each image, for Spenser is trying to show bright and various colors which also flash with iridescence. In the peacock's train he finds these qualities along with precisely "distinguished" arrangement "passing farre/ All Painters skill"; "ey-spotted" calls up the mysterious varying brightness of the eye's light, and is an exact figure for the peacock's markings, which produce flashing white light from a luminescent black center. This combination of star and rainbow is reminiscent of the moon-rainbow in the passage I have just discussed from *Colin Clouts Come Home Againe*. The stanza is a tightly closed unit, ending as it does with a couplet the imagery of which includes and amplifies the separate metaphors that precede it.

Clarion's wings remain the subject, directly or indirectly, throughout six more stanzas in which the original image is first expanded and then mythologized. Not even Cupid "Beares in his wings so manie a changefull token," and the ladies at court "wisht that two such fannes, so silken soft,/ And golden faire, her Loue would her prouide" (101 and 107-108). Finally, Spenser invents a myth to explain the butterfly's origin as Astery, the nymph of Venus who raised envy in her companions by gathering more flowers than they. She was turned into a butterfly when they persuaded Venus, "Not yet vnmindfull, how not long agoe/ Her sonne to *Psyche* secrete loue did beare" (130-131), that Cupid had secretly helped in the gathering. The myth explains the colors in the butterfly's wings, since

> all those flowres, with which so plenteouslie
> Her lap she filled had, that bred her spight,
> She placed in her wings, for memorie
> Of her pretended crime, though crime none were:
> Since which that flie them in her wings doth beare.
> (140-144)

Spenser accounts for the spider Aragnoll's hatred of the butterfly with a story based upon Ovid's account of a tapestry-weaving contest between Arachne and Minerva.[20] The emphasis of Ovid's story is altered, and Minerva wins not by force but by weaving an astonishingly lifelike butterfly into the scene of her own debate with Neptune over Athens; Spenser uses that pictorial energy charged into his own earlier image of Clarion to support the victory. Otherwise, he seems to be describing an encounter between Arachne and Minerva which might be taken for a storytelling contest instead of a tapestry-weaving competition were it not for the use of such words as "figur'd" and "pictur'd," as well as the device of hinging the outcome on an image of the butterfly and a brief description of one tapestry border. The ecphrastic writing in this tale is so skillful and self-conscious that Spenser seems to be commenting upon the limitations of ecphrasis by employing it.

Arachne's tapestry is of Europa and the Bull as they move out through the sea, "so liuely seene,/ That it true Sea, and true Bull ye would weene" (279-280). Some of the details in Arachne's depiction, particularly of Europa, are extremely fine and lively:

> She seem'd still backe vnto the land to looke,
> And her play-fellowes aide to call, and feare
> The dashing of the waues, that vp she tooke
> Her daintie feete, and garments gathered neare:
> But (Lord) how she in euerie member shooke,
> When as the land she saw no more appeare,
> But a wilde wildernes of waters deepe:
> Then gan she greatly to lament and weepe.
>
> Before the Bull she pictur'd winged Loue,
> With his yong brother Sport, light fluttering
> Vpon the waues, as each had been a Doue;
> The one his bowe and shafts, the other Spring

[20] *Metamorphoses*, 6.1-145; see *Variorum*, 8.400-403.

A burning Teade about his head did moue,
As in their Syres new loue both triumphing:
And manie Nymphes about them flocking round,
And manie *Tritons*, which their hornes did sound.

(281-296)

Here, as so often in ecphrastic writing, the "picture" is a narrative interlaced with descriptive detail. Tapestries using the continuous narrative technique can of course tell stories, and we are perhaps to imagine two Europa figures in Arachne's; but Spenser uses the singular in his introduction (280), and the one pair of *putti* he mentions would have to accompany two representations of Europa. The passage is a forceful narrative, but it is not visually precise. I cannot agree with Renwick, who says that this scene seems "to suggest that Spenser knew a good picture of the Rape of Europa."[21]

There is nothing so forceful in Minerva's tapestry, and, whereas we can imagine Arachne's story unfolding as she weaves, Minerva's is shown in narratively climactic order. The gods "doo sit around in royall state,/ And *Ioue* in midst with awfull Maiestie" (307-308). Neptune "strikes the rockes with his three-forked mace;/ Whenceforth issues a warlike steed in sight" (315-316). And Pallas "smote the ground, the which streight foorth did yield/ A fruitfull Olyue tree, with berries spredd" (325-326). This is a fairly dull picture, and at this point it seems to me incontestable that Arachne should

---

[21] *Complaints*, p. 254. Spenser, here as in his four lines on Europa in the House of Busyrane (3.11.30), synthesizes a number of literary sources: see Douglas Bush, *Mythology and the Renaissance Tradition in English Poetry* (Minneapolis, 1932), pp. 108-109. As Arachne's subject was extremely popular in the Renaissance, Spenser might have seen it pictured, but then the pictures were partly inspired by literary sources. For example, Erwin Panofsky, *The Life and Art of Albrecht Dürer* (Princeton, 1955), p. 34, cites Poliziano's *La Giostra* as a source of Dürer's drawing of Europa.

win—if only for her superior choice of subject. However, Minerva adds the butterfly to her olive tree:

> Emongst those leaues she made a Butterflie,
> With excellent deuice and wondrous slight,
> Fluttring among the Oliues wantonly,
> That seem'd to liue, so like it was in sight:
> The veluet nap which on his wings doth lie,
> The silken downe with which his backe is dight,
> His broad outstretched hornes, his hayrie thies,
> His glorious colours, and his glistering eies.
>
> (329-336)

Whereupon Arachne "stood astonied long, . . . And by her silence, signe of one dismaid,/ The victorie did yeeld her as her share" (339-342). We are told that Minerva won, but rhetorically the poem must lead us to the belief that she deserved her victory. I think that comparison of the tapestries alone, even considering the added butterfly, does not carry such conviction to the audience; Minerva loses with a very similar picture in Ovid, and the added butterfly is not enough to counter the remarkable energy and detail of Arachne's tapestry. Still, the victory is convincing because Spenser has already shown this butterfly with considerable pictorial force earlier in the *Muiopotmos*. The carefully balanced economy of such a short narrative poem makes repetition of the original unnecessary and undesirable, so lines that sketch and recall the first image make it function again. Arachne's own rage transforms her into a spider, and as Aragnoll's mother she indirectly becomes a figure in the main action; Spenser's return to the story of Aragnoll and Clarion is in fact so abrupt and ambiguous that momentarily the two spiders merge (353-354). "The Fate of the Butterflie" is to be represented so realistically in art that it can be killed in fact.

Pictorial Vision

The *Epithalamion* is still richer in visual materials than the *Muiopotmos*—rich enough that we seem intended to have an impression of almost continuous vision. In part this is because many traditional topoi for epithalamia are natural occasions for the enumeration of sights, and the festive character of such a poem makes plentiful enrichment and elaboration not only rhetorically possible but desirable. Such events in an epithalamion as the dawning of the wedding day, the awakening of the Bride, the process of attiring her, her first appearance and the reactions to it, the couple's appearance in the temple or church, the wedding itself, the feasting, the evening, the bedding of the Bride, and the dawn of a new morning invite a richness of visual reference.[22] In Spenser's *Epithalamion* virtually no such opportunity passes unrealized, and there are other visual touches besides. The sheer density of visual figures and descriptions is impressive.

A few examples should be enough to convey an immediate feeling of the poem's visual preoccupation, potentiality, and sumptuousness. Nymphs are told to come from the rivers, forests, and neighboring seas,

> Al with gay girlands goodly wel beseene.
> And let them also with them bring in hand
> Another gay girland
> For my fayre loue of lillyes and of roses,
> Bound trueloue wize with a blew silke riband.
> And let them make great store of bridale poses,
> And let them eeke bring store of other flowers
> To deck the bridale bowers.   (40-47)

---

[22] Thomas M. Greene, "Spenser and the Epithalamic Convention," *CL*, ix (1957), 215-228, enumerates the conventional topoi, compares other epithalamia with Spenser's, and discusses the effect of Spenser's many departures from convention.

Pictorialism in the Minor Poems

The Nymphs of Mulla and those "likewise which keepe the rushy lake" are commanded to

> Bynd vp the locks the which hang scatterd light,
> And in his waters which your mirror make,
> Behold your faces as the christall bright,
> That when you come whereas my loue doth lie,
> No blemish she may spie.   (62-66)

When the bride appears there is, of course, a particular profuseness of visual reference:

> Loe where she comes along with portly pace,
> Lyke Phoebe from her chamber of the East,
> Arysing forth to run her mighty race,
> Clad all in white, that seemes a virgin best.
> So well it her beseemes that ye would weene
> Some angell she had beene.
> Her long loose yellow locks lyke golden wyre,
> Sprinckled with perle, and perling flowres a tweene,
> Doe lyke a golden mantle her attyre,
> And being crowned with a girland greene,
> Seeme lyke some mayden Queene.   (148-158)

Details are important as well as large blocks of description and elaborate figures. The verbal pun on "perle" is also a visual pun, the verbal juxtaposition a visual conjunction which causes us to revisualize a metaphor so familiar that it was almost dead even in the Renaissance.[23] Because of this sub-miniature, almost Focused, image these three lines on the

[23] See *OED*, 7, "To form pearl-like drops or beads"; the citation is from *Colin Clout*, 507: "With siluer deaw vpon the roses pearling." Other examples from Spenser are, "Few perling drops from her faire lampes of light" (*FQ*, 5.9.50); and "Vpon the perled grasse to make their feast" (*Colin Clout*, 607).

Bride's "long loose yellow locks" approach pictorial force. In a series of images the next stanza calls "merchants daughters" to observe the Bride's beauty; such imagery originates in the *Song of Songs*, a work which Spenser must have taken as an epithalamion:[24]

> Her goodly eyes lyke Saphyres shining bright,
> Her forehead yuory white,
> Her cheekes lyke apples which the sun hath rudded,
> Her lips lyke cherryes charming men to byte,
> Her brest like to a bowle of creame vncrudded,
> Her paps lyke lyllies budded,
> Her snowie necke lyke to a marble towre,
> And all her body like a pallace fayre,
> Ascending vppe with many a stately stayre,
> To honors seat and chastities sweet bowre.
>
> (171-180)

One critic calls this imagery "emblematic," but technically it fits Puttenham's definition of the figure Icon.[25] Toward the end of the series especially, the imagery's visual force is entirely subordinate to its symbolism.

These and many other passages contribute to the impression that the *Epithalamion* is a poem almost unparalleled in profuseness of visual reference, yet it contains only one marginally pictorial image. Spenser places this image strategically at the center of a work whose world is, as Thomas M. Greene says, "concentric": "The poem begins and ends with the widest perspective; at the center of the poem, during the ceremony, the focus has narrowed to the couple itself. Immediately be-

---

[24] Hallett Smith, "The Use of Conventions in Spenser's Minor Poems," p. 140; and Israel Baroway, "The Imagery of Spenser and the *Song of Songs*," *JEGP*, xxxiii (1934), 31-33.

[25] Smith, p. 140; and *The Arte of English Poesie*, ed. Gladys Doidge Willcock and Alice Walker (Cambridge, 1936), pp. 241-243; also *Variorum*, 8.474.

fore and after the ceremony the focus includes the 'social con-
text.' The opening, with its perspective into the past, is bal-
anced by the concluding perspective into the future" (p. 228).
Appropriately, a Focused image appears as the Bride stands
before the altar at the moment of the speaker's greatest de-
sire to *show* her to the world—the stanza even begins with
"Behold":

> Behold whiles she before the altar stands
> Hearing the holy priest that to her speakes
> And blesseth her with his two happy hands,
> How the red roses flush vp in her cheekes,
> And the pure snow with goodly vermill stayne,
> Like crimsin dyde in grayne,
> That euen th'Angels which continually,
> About the sacred Altare doe remaine,
> Forget their seruice and about her fly,
> Ofte peeping in her face that seemes more fayre,
> The more they on it stare.
>
> (223-233)

The basic pattern of Focused imagery is present: three accounts
of the Bride's flushing cheeks followed by a shift to the mytho-
logical or supernatural. Focused images often proceed by
negation, antithesis, or discord; perhaps because it is concord-
ant this one is less strikingly pictorial. Spenser uses conven-
tional metaphors to show the Bride's cheeks and to comment
upon conventionality much as he does when Britomart is
revealed to Artegall during their combat in Book Four (see
Chapters Two and Three above). The blushing cheeks are
shown in three diminishingly iconic lines. First, "red roses,"
then "pure snow with goodly vermill stayne," and finally
"Like crimsin dyde in grayne." The last line is an exact rep-
resentation of the color as well as a comment upon the Bride's
purity and sincerity of emotion: "dyde in grayne" means dyed

in kermes, the finest crimson coloring, and also, by a meta-
phorical extension common in the Renaissance, sincere or
unchangeable (*OED*, iii.io.a-c). Finally, instead of drawing
a mythological comparison, the poet invokes the supernatural
to witness this extraordinary sight; he implies that the Bride's
beauty is so remarkable that it inspires life in ordinary, static
works of art such as the angels wrought about the altar.[26]

The *Epithalamion* is a work rich in visual reference, but
the one Focused image it contains does not dominate our
imagination of the poem as the many pictorial images in *The
Faerie Queene*, the modest image of the butterfly in *Muiopot-
mos*, or the image of two swans in the *Prothalamion* dominate
their poems. The combined descriptions and images associ-
ated with the Bride might constitute such a picture, but they
seem too weak to emerge in relief from the profusion of
Spenser's visual materials. This is not necessarily a fault, for
the *Epithalamion* is a festive poem which seeks special effects;
it employs the conventions of a genre, but makes its own rules
and convinces us of their inevitability. The long and emphati-
cally closed stanza form, which helps, just as in the *Protha-
lamion*, to differentiate the masses of rich detail by establish-
ing a series of discrete units concentrating upon one subject,
is only one example of Spenser's modification of the conven-
tional form. The theories proposed in this study can help us
to analyze the poem, but they cannot fully explain its effect.

I have already discussed in Chapter Three the emblematic
function of Focused and Framed pictorial imagery when the
Prothalamion swans appear, but other important features of
the work deserve mention. The *Prothalamion* is Spenser's
only minor poem in which spaces are created and juxtaposed

[26] *Variorum*, 8.477-478: "The ancient liturgies of the Church show
that Angels are present at Holy Mass and that they join with the con-
gregation in singing the Sanctus. . . . Often in churches the door of
the Tabernacle on the Altar is adorned with figures of Angels in
adoration, in imitation of the Tabernacle of the Old Testament."

as they are in *The Faerie Queene*. As in *The Faerie Queene*, the spaces are usually created by the activity within them. At the beginning, "in a Meadow, by the Riuers side" is "a Flocke of *Nymphes*" gathering flowers; a catalog of the flowers they gather replaces description of the meadow. Then the "two Swannes of goodly hewe,/ Come softly swimming downe along the Lee" (37-38); they are presented in a series of spectacular images of whiteness, the last of which again reminds us of the river setting:

> So purely white they were,
> That euen the gentle streame, the which them bare,
> Seem'd foule to them, and bad his billowes spare
> To wet their silken feathers, least they might
> Soyle their fayre plumes with water not so fayre.
>
> (46-50)

There is no sense of spatial continuity or scale between meadow and stream until the nymphs, now with "Flowers their fill," run "all in haste, to see that siluer brood,/ As they came floating on the Christal Flood" (56-57). The balance of stanza four is devoted to the nymphs' rapt amazement, and only in five do nymphs and swans momentarily become actors in a single scene:

> Then forth they all out of their baskets drew
> Great store of Flowers, the honour of the field,
> That to the sense did fragrant odours yield,
> All which vpon those goodly Birds they threw,
> And all the Waues did strew,
> That like old *Peneus* Waters they did seeme,
> When downe along by pleasant *Tempes* shore
> Scattred with Flowres, through *Thessaly* they streeme.
>
> (73-80)

A song from one of the nymphs marks the end of this scene.

In the transitional stanza seven where the swans proceed to
scene two in London, the movement is similar to the spatially
indeterminate transitions in *The Faerie Queene*: "So forth
those ioyous Birdes did passe along,/ Adowne the Lee, that
to them murmurde low" (114-115). The river makes "his
streame run slow" in tribute and all of the water birds "en-
ranged well,/ Did on those two attend," but there is no refer-
ence to the shore, so the transition is formal and rhetorical
rather than spatial—even though the swans are supposed to
be moving along a familiar and geographically existent river.

When, "at length they all to mery *London* came," the
topography of the poem suddenly becomes explicit. The birds
pass the "bricky towres" of the Inner Temple and come to
Essex House, which was directly adjacent on the former
grounds of the Outer Temple. Spenser refers to his former
association with the house when it was Leicester's, and to its
present occupancy by Essex, whom he digresses to praise in
stanza nine.[27] Then,

> From those high Towers, this noble Lord issuing,
> Like Radiant *Hesper* when his golden hayre
> In th' *Ocean* billowes he hath Bathed fayre,
> Descended to the Riuers open vewing,
> With a great traine ensuing.
> Aboue the rest were goodly to bee seene
> Two gentle Knights of louely face and feature.
>
> . . . .
>
> They two forth pacing to the Riuers side,
> Receiued those two faire Brides, their Loues delight.
>
> (163-176)

[27] Charles L. Kingsford, "Essex House, formerly Leicester House
and Exeter Inn," *Archaeologia*, LXXIII (1923), 1-54, gives a history of
the house and an inventory of Leicester's goods in the house. He says,
pp. 10-11, that Spenser stayed at Essex House on his return to London
in 1595 and wrote the *Prothalamion* for a double marriage there on
November 8 of that year. See also *Variorum*, 8.495-496.

This final scene, like the first in the poem, ends as river and shore are joined by an action—now literally real as well as poetically meaningful.

In the *Prothalamion* Spenser uses pictorial techniques to combine myth and reality into a single fragmented and highly formalized artifact from which actual lovers and brides emerge only a few lines before the final echo of his refrain. He connects well-known places and an actual festive marriage with a mythologized compliment; real places and people become allegorical representations imagined in a shattered pictorial world where strange spatial organization puts the familiar at a slight distance, and where pictorial vividness makes myth seem more familiar. Spenser's pictorial techniques, Focusing, Framing, and Scanning, help to keep our response to an exaggerated compliment under perfect control. Because of the references to actual topography, Spenser's management of fragmented space in the *Prothalamion* does not produce the impression of visionary experience so prominent in *The Faerie Queene*. Indeed, there is slight spatial continuity at the end of each of the *Prothalamion*'s two main sections, an effect appropriate in occasional poetry intended to deliver a specific compliment. However, in no other minor poem does Spenser employ the pictorial techniques I discuss in this study at all as he does in *The Faerie Queene*. Many of the other minor poems are emblematic or intentionally epigrammatic in their brevity; others are uncongenial to pictorial effects because of their argumentative character or plainness of style. The more expansive mythmaking and celebratory genres of poetry, which invite amplification, seem to be those most hospitable to pictorialism. Larger pictorial forms of course require contexts more generous than those the lyric ordinarily provides.

Illusion in the Bowre of Blisse

It is not surprising that the expansiveness and formal openness of *The Faerie Queene*, as well as the mythmaking so important to Spenser's presentation of its world, encourage the development of many pictorial effects—some of which familiarize us with Faerie Land while others place it just beyond our reach. Narrative in epic and Romance traditionally offers a poet occasions for the display of descriptive and pictorial imagery, but Spenser is especially preoccupied with images. A Spenserian hero is likely at any moment to find that his survival depends upon correct interpretation of images confronting him. As readers we find ourselves similarly, though less urgently, confronted. In this sense, not in the sense of dramatic empathy, we share the hero's quest. Britomart's quest actually begins with a surprising image, not with a sudden feeling or a dramatic encounter, and like Guyon's it ends with the destruction of dangerous illusions forged by a vicious artist. In fact, Guyon's entire quest is presented as a series of challenges to the hero's interpretive powers.

There are many references to *The Faerie Queene* in previous chapters where I have discussed different pictorial techniques. Now, it seems appropriate to conclude by showing all of the techniques combined in Spenser's most sustained piece of pictorial writing, the Bowre of Blisse (2.12.42-87). Like the *Epithalamion*, the Bowre of Blisse episode is rich in visual reference. But unlike the *Epithalamion* which attempts, with partial success I think, to embody an entire visual world, the Bowre, with controlled profusion, stimulates in the reader's imagination the impression of interlocking tableaux not of a spatial continuum. In such a long passage, constructed from descriptive materials as well as pictorial images, lateral Scanning is of course the general technique.

The Bowre of Blisse is in "A place pickt out by choice of best aliue,/ That natures worke by art can imitate" (2.12.42). Immediately, two opposite impressions of the Bowre's surrounding fence confront us, and we begin to understand the mimetic powers of these artists "best aliue":

Goodly it was enclosed round about,
Aswell their entred guestes to keepe within,
As those vnruly beasts to hold without;
Yet was the fence thereof but weake and thin;
Nought feard their force, that fortilage to win,
But wisedomes powre, and temperaunces might,
By which the mightiest things efforced bin.

(2.12.43)

The viewer, whose approaching movement is clearly implicit, first sees and glosses a strong enclosure, then a frail fence; the purpose of this illusion, like the others Guyon encounters, is to confuse the understanding through the senses. To perceive this fence as a "goodly" enclosure is, under the spell of illusion, to misconceive the true threat of this place; it is equally dangerous to believe, having accurately *seen* a "weake and thin" barrier, that simple force can win it. From the beginning Spenser shows that our responses to the Bowre's challenge must be a dialectic between precise visual apprehension and accurate "seeing" in the broadest sense. Acrasia entraps those who rely exclusively upon either sensuous perception or rigid precepts. Guyon alternates between these extremes, and so would be in serious danger without the Palmer's aid.

At the entrance "the gate was wrought of substaunce light,/ Rather for pleasure, then for battery or fight":

Yt framed was of precious yuory,
That seemd a worke of admirable wit;
And therein all the famous history
Of *Iason* and *Medaea* was ywrit;
Her mighty charmes, her furious louing fit,
His goodly conquest of the golden fleece,
His falsed faith, and loue too lightly flit,
The wondred *Argo*, which in venturous peece
First through the *Euxine* seas bore all the flowr of
    Greece.

Ye might haue seene the frothy billowes fry
Vnder the ship, as thorough them she went,
That seemd the waues were into yuory,
Or yuory into the waues were sent;
And other where the snowy substaunce sprent
With vermell, like the boyes bloud therein shed,
A piteous spectacle did represent,
And otherwhiles with gold besprinkeled;
Yt seemd th'enchaunted flame, which did *Creüsa* wed.

(2.12.44-45)

In a similar context Tasso devotes seven stanzas of *Gerusa-
lemme liberata* to stories represented in the gates of Armida's
palace, but after an introduction he says little about the artistry
of the gates: they are silver on golden hinges and fine work-
manship makes the figures seem alive except for their lack
of speech.

Le porte qui d'effigiato argento
su i cardini stridean di lucid'oro.
Fermar ne le figure il guardo intento,
ché vinta la materia è dal lavoro:
manca il parlar, di vivo altro non chiedi;
né manca questo ancor, s'a gli occhi credi.

(16.2.3-8)

The door leaves fram'd of carved silver plate
Upon their golden hinges turn and twine:
They stay'd to view this work of wit and state,
The workmanship excell'd the substance fine,
For all the shapes in that rich metal wrought,
Save speech, of living bodies wanted nought.

There are two lines of conclusion in stanza seven, but other-
wise the artist's skillful use of materials is only indirectly

Tasso's subject.[28] Spenser and Tasso both put stories on their portals which represent the power of passionate female magicians over heroes. Spenser devotes only two stanzas to his gates, in which he emphasizes remarkable visual effects at least as much as the legend of Jason and Medea.[29]

The first of Spenser's two stanzas is a tight catalog of scenes represented on the gates, and they appear roughly in the order of the legend's chief episodes. The Argo is seen last, as if represented in a separate panel of the gates. The second stanza also alludes to these parts of the story, especially to the appearance of Jason's ship; but more importantly, as Upton observes, it refers in passing to the stories of Creusa and "the murdered Absyrtes, whom his sister Medea tore limb from limb, and scattered them in various places, that her father might be stopt in his pursuit after her, whilst he was employed in gathering the mangled and dispersed limbs of his son." Upton says that Spenser alludes to Absyrtes in "the boyes bloud therein shed," and not to Medea's "murdering her own sons; whom likewise she slew, when with her inchanted present she burnt her rival Creusa. This present was, as some say, a nuptial crown; others, a wedding robe."[30]

The purpose of stanza forty-five seems to be to show transformations of natural substances by art and to represent through images the eerie uncertainties and illusions of the Bowre of Blisse. This stanza represents the sensuous impres-

---

[28] With the possible exception of 16.4.5, where "d'oro fiammeggia l'onda" can be taken literally or figuratively.

[29] Of course the story is far from unimportant. Henry Gibbons Lotspeich, *Classical Mythology in the Poetry of Edmund Spenser* (Princeton, 1932), pp. 38-39, says that Natalis Comes, 6.7, "affords an explanation for the use of this myth in connection with Acrasia. In his moral interpretation, Jason's love for Medea (a kind of Circe, like Acrasia) is giving in to 'voluptatum desiderium'; he who was by nature wise and good was dominated by lust and 'ad turpitudinem cupiditatibus moderatur.'"

[30] *Variorum*, 2.372.

sion of an illusion, and through its diction reminds us that the illusion is a product of craft. The viewer recognizes waves, blood, or flames, yet knows that they are created out of ivory, vermilion, and gold. Progression is orderly in stanza forty-four, but in the next stanza Spenser is concerned to represent the randomness of a viewer's encounter with an illusionistic work of art and uses the indefinite transitions "and other where" or "and otherwhiles." Spenser's casual subordinate treatment of elements from the Medea story in stanza forty-five works like Focused imagery to build an impression of sensuous discovery; these scenes are noticed because of the imagined craftsman's skillful use of materials. In particular the last scene's introduction with "otherwhiles" makes its appearance seem almost accidental, as if it came to the attention not as part of the story but because of the ivory's transformation when "with gold besprinkled;/ Yt seemd th'enchaunted flame, which did *Creüsa* wed." These last lines show a precise sequence of pictorial realization: from the golden material, to a first apprehension of the illusion of "th'enchaunted flame," to full perception in the final metaphor of Creusa enveloped with the flames from Medea's poisoned gift.

In the porch Guyon and the Palmer encounter a seated figure whose appearance is described briefly. He is the Genius Agdistes. Spenser presents him in an inverted emblem which brings us to a full conceptual understanding of the figure's identity and significance before reinforcing our knowledge with a stanza that shows his visible attributes. This inverted emblem is conceptually more explicit and visually less complex than that one I have already discussed (in Chapter Four) of Ariadne's crown on Mount Acidale (6.10.13); there are structural similarities, but the slight description of Agdistes bears a gloss of two stanzas over it instead of a few lines. It appears that Agdistes' attributes alone cannot account for Guyon's rough treatment of him:

With diuerse flowres he daintily was deckt,
And strowed round about, and by his side
A might Mazer bowle of wine was set,
As if it had to him bene sacrifide;
Wherewith all new-come guests he gratifide:
So did he eke Sir *Guyon* passing by:
But he his idle curtesie defide,
And ouerthrew his bowle disdainfully;
And broke his staffe, with which he charmed
     semblants sly.   (2.12.49)[31]

Especially because of its inverted organization, the emblem of Agdistes breaks spatial continuity between the gates and what is behind them. This expository presentation of Agdistes contributes significantly to our sense of spatial disorientation at the entrance to the Bowre of Blisse. Spenser's treatment of space here and elsewhere in *The Faerie Queene* is much affected by his "avowedly expository" design, a phrase used by Robert M. Durling in his comparison of Spenser's exordia with Ariosto's.[32] The Genius is "in the Porch" (2.12.46), yet the "fence" is described and the image of the gates fully presented before he is even noticed. The gates presumably are also in the porch, but there is no hint that they are part of

---

[31] The iconography is concisely explained by Upton, *Variorum*, 2.376: "They worshiped this God Genius, with libations of wine, and with garlands of flowers. So Natalis Comes, 4.3, 'Huic Genio cum sacra fierent flores complures humi spargebantur, vinumque illi in pateris offerabatur.' Horace, *Ars Poetica*, 210:

               Vinoque diurno
     Placari Genius festis impune diebus."

For more interpretive material see *Variorum*, 2.377; and especially C. S. Lewis, *The Allegory of Love* (New York, 1936), pp. 361-363.

[32] *The Figure of the Poet in Renaissance Epic* (Cambridge, Mass., 1965), p. 219. Durling says that in Spenser "the relation between the reflections and the events is reversed—the reflections come first and the events second."

the same spatial continuum as the Genius Agdistes. He mate-
rializes just in time to be explained and cast down. This fig-
ure appearing suddenly in a prearranged architectural setting
seems to be conceived like the *imagines agentes* or memory
images of the classical and medieval tradition.[33]

Immediately after throwing down the Genius, Guyon and
the Palmer are in an empty space:

> Thus being entred, they behold around
> A large and spacious plaine, on euery side
> Strowed with pleasauns, whose faire grassy ground
> Mantled with greene, and goodly beautifide
> With all the ornaments of *Floraes* pride,
> Wherewith her mother Art, as halfe in scorne
> Of niggard Nature, like a pompous bride
> Did decke her, and too lauishly adorne,
> When forth from virgin bowre she comes in th'early
>   morne.
>
> Thereto the Heauens alwayes Iouiall,
> Lookt on them louely, still in stedfast state,
> Ne suffred storme nor frost on them to fall,
> Their tender buds or leaues to violate,
> Nor scorching heat, nor cold intemperate
> T'afflict the creatures, which therein did dwell.
>
> (2.12.50-51)

A long series of comparisons with ideal places in ancient
myth and with other garden paradises, including Eden, dif-
fuses the pictorial effect (2.12.52), even though the abrupt
beginning, and later the sudden jump at stanza fifty-three
into Guyon's mind, would otherwise mark this a spatially
coherent Framed image at a juncture in the action. Also, the

---

[33] See Chapter Four above; and Frances A. Yates, *The Art of Memory*
(Chicago and London, 1966), pp. 55ff, 92, *et passim*.

reversal of expectations at Guyon's rejection of "that sweet place" when he "passed forth, and lookt still forward right,/ Bridling his will, and maistering his might" (2.12.53) forces the confused reader back for a fresh scrutiny of the image. Framing is provided for scenery that never quite appears, and the "spacious plaine" remains a visually indefinite transition in which much description is devoted to the climate. Spenser maintains a consistent poetic texture so that we can easily be deceived as we Scan through the passage. For the first time, in the Bowre we momentarily follow a lure that Guyon avoids. His sudden rejection is explained not by what we see, but, it seems, by the dark resonance of mythological figures and places that are associated with the plain.[34]

There is another break in spatial continuity as Guyon goes on, indeterminately, "Till that he came vnto another gate" (2.12.53). This is made not of ivory and gold, but "With boughes and braunches, which did broad dilate/ Their clasping armes, in wanton wreathings intricate" (2.12.53). The porch before this gate has been made, or has grown, out of the same greenery:

> So fashioned a Porch with rare deuice,
> Archt ouer head with an embracing vine,
> Whose bounches hanging downe, seemed to entice
> All passers by, to tast their lushious wine,
> And did themselues into their hands incline,
> As freely offering to be gathered:
> Some deepe empurpled as the *Hyacine*,
> Some as the Rubine, laughing sweetly red,
> Some like faire Emeraudes, not yet well ripened.

[34] On Flora, Rhodope, and Daphne see *Variorum*, 2.378-379. On Ida, F. A. Wright, ed. *Lemprière's Classical Dictionary* (London, 1949), p. 293. Eden requires no reference. In this respect Parnassus does not seem to fit the context.

And them amongst, some were of burnisht gold,
So made by art, to beautifie the rest,
Which did themselues emongst the leaues enfold,
As lurking from the vew of couetous guest,
That the weake bowes, with so rich load opprest,
Did bow adowne, as ouer-burdened.

(2.12.54-55)

The Focused image in these lines on the grapes employs a brief descriptive list as a base from which to represent visual ambiguity and finely wrought illusion. Grapes that hang down as enticingly as these invite examination, and at first they appear to be a heightened variety of natural grapes with fully ripe, almost ripe, and still green fruit in each cluster. The three kinds are compared in similes with three gems, the most artificial of natural things. However, inspection reveals that among these grapes "some were of burnisht gold"; simile is suddenly replaced by simple statement, and because of this wrought fruit the viewer's figurative perception of the other grapes as jewels has to be reexamined. Perhaps all of the grapes are "made by art" and are in fact jewels shaped to look like clustered fruit. The eye suddenly seems incapable of making necessary distinctions, and "the artificial . . . infects all around it with its artificiality. The real grapes, compared to gems, suddenly acquire an artificial quality which is increased when they are juxtaposed with the truly artificial gold grapes."[35] The visual ambiguity is probably even greater than this interpretation implies, and we join Guyon in a test of visual discrimination. What is real and what is illusion? The eye cannot tell, for even as they are squeezed these grapes produce a strange juice which seems not to stain the fingers of Excesse:

[35] A. Bartlett Giamatti, *The Earthly Paradise and the Renaissance Epic* (Princeton, 1966), p. 272.

In her left hand a Cup of gold she held,
And with her right the riper fruit did reach,
Whose sappy liquor, that with fulnesse sweld,
Into her cup she scruzd, with daintie breach
Of her fine fingers, without fowle empeach,
That so faire wine-presse made the wine more sweet.

(2.12.56)[36]

We begin to perceive that these grapes are part of a nature so heightened by art that nature becomes merely a basic material of visual trickery. In fact, not only do the golden grapes "beautifie the rest," the entire architecture of the porch *depends* quite literally upon their effect: their artificial weight, not natural abundance, is the reason "That the weake bowes, with so rich load opprest,/ Did bow adowne, as ouer-burdened."

Only after examining the grapes have we learned that "Vnder that Porch a comely dame did rest." Spenser's presentation of experience in the Bowre continues to be fractional, and like the Genius this "dame" seems to materialize just in time for her role. Unlike him she acts within the setting that we already have seen in the previous frame, and squeezes the ripe grapes into her golden cup. She is shown in one stanza (2.12.56), and in the next Guyon "The cup to ground did violently cast." The two stanzas balance one another like a pair of pendant emblems—"Excesse" and the "Fall of Excesse"—although neither is a pictorial image. The stanza presenting the lady does not contain action in any normal sense, since she eternally squeezes grapes into her golden cup and at the same time eternally offers it to the passing stranger. We may imagine her, in the continuous narrative style, as one of those figures "presented in a kind of double exposure that

---

[36] I think that the extremely ambiguous phrase, "without fowle empeach," means "without foul injury, damage or detriment" (*OED*, 2) rather than "without foul hindrance" (*OED*, 1). It can refer either to "fine fingers" or to the wine itself.

requires it to function in two successive roles."[37] The narrative is all compressed into stanza fifty-seven, where Guyon takes the cup and breaks it; finally the name of the figure, Excesse, is mentioned for the first time and Guyon "nought regarding her displeasure forward goth."

The next scene in the Bowre of Blisse appears immediately: "There the most daintie Paradise on ground,/ It selfe doth offer to his sober eye" (2.12.58). There is a brief scenic catalog of "flowres," "trees," "dales," "hilles," and "groues" (2.12.58), but the following stanzas approximate an extended perspective where things and actions are set in determinate spatial relationships to one another. Scenic elements are given summarily, then a detailed account of the fountain in "midst of all" and of the jasper-bottomed pool or lake around it where "naked Damzelles" display themselves to Guyon. Spenser appears to want this centerpiece, Guyon's most alluring temptation in the Bowre, to be illusionistic even if its spatial connections with surrounding scenes are tenuous. The verse is laden with descriptive detail as well as with pictorial and near-pictorial imagery. The descriptive material fuses with the pictorial imagery into an unbroken sequence.

The first stanza depicting the fountain is remarkable for its precise detail. The fountain, most certainly crystal although the material is not named, is

> Of richest substaunce, that on earth might bee,
> So pure and shiny, that the siluer flood
> Through euery channell running one might see;
> Most goodly it with curious imageree
> Was ouer-wrought, and shapes of naked boyes,
> Of which some seemd with liuely iollitee,
> To fly about, playing their wanton toyes,
> Whilest others did them selues embay in liquid ioyes.
>
> (2.12.60)

[37] Joseph B. Dallett, "Ideas of Sight in *The Faerie Queene*," *ELH*, xxvii (1960), 100, and n. 31.

These lines exactly represent a visual phenomenon; the fountain is shaped of a substance so clear that another clear substance can be seen running through it. In addition, some of the crystal is carved or etched with figures that seem to move because of light sparkling on the water. Spenser captures with his ambiguous "it" the eye's inability to distinguish accurately between the "siluer flood" and the fountain's "ouer-wrought" crystal channels in which it runs. Then with the "liuely" figures he refers to the shifting reflections of light in cut crystal which holds moving water.

The following stanza is a special kind of Focused image in which the effect of a sight upon the speaker reflects with pictorial force the visual complexity and persuasiveness of an illusion:

> And ouer all, of purest gold was spred,
> A trayle of yuie in his natiue hew:
> For the rich mettall was so coloured,
> That wight, who did not well auis'd it vew,
> Would surely deeme it to be yuie trew:
> Low his lasciuious armes adown did creepe,
> That themselues dipping in the siluer dew,
> Their fleecy flowres they tenderly did steepe,
> Which drops of Christall seemd for wantones to weepe.
>
> (2.12.61)

We are told that only by judicious inspection can anyone discover this ivy really to be made of gold; it is "in his natiue hew," and we "would surely deeme it to be yuie trew." The speaker knows these things, yet he appears to be deluded by the imitation ivy as he tells how illusionistic it is: at first the ivy, which is probably a symbol of lust,[38] has "lasciuious armes," but then its flowers are "fleecy" and "tenderly did steepe" in the "siluer dew." Finally the ivy is connected visually with the previous image of a transparent fountain, and,

[38] C. W. Lemmi, *Variorum*, 2.382.

with light personification, the flowers "drops of Christall seemd for wantones to weepe." The false ivy is so realistic that it lures even the poet who knows its falsehood momentarily to speak of it with empathy. Because the eye is deceived, the intellect still will not believe what it knows to be true. This paradox, which is central to the Bowre's challenge and to Spenser's distrust of its illusionism, allies our experience with Guyon's and enlists our imaginative sympathy as he approaches his greatest test.

Spenser has begun with the fountain "in the midst of all" (2.12.60). He moves outward to its carved ornamentation, to the false ivy, and next to the surrounding "ample lauer": "All pau'd beneath with Iaspar shining bright,/ That seemd the fountaine in that sea did sayle vpright" (2.12.62). Then all is brilliantly ordered in perspective. The scene is set for Guyon's temptation by a designer who commands the powers Sidney attributes to art in *An Apology for Poetry*, but with vicious rather than high moral purposes.

> And all the margent round about was set,
> With shady Laurell trees, thence to defend
> The sunny beames, which on the billowes bet,
> And those which therein bathed, mote offend.
> As *Guyon* hapned by the same to wend,
> Two naked Damzelles he therein espyde,
> Which therein bathing, seemed to contend,
> And wrestle wantonly, ne car'd to hyde,
> Their dainty parts from vew of any, which them eyde.
>
> (2.12.63)

The laurel trees establish a perimeter, the tonality of light is defined, and Guyon is placed as a spectator glimpsing "therein." Here, without the Palmer, in the Bowre's most artfully contrived setting will be Guyon's severest trial. The "naked Damzelles" seem to appear just to play out their roles for

Illusion in the Bowre of Blisse

Guyon, and he spies them from precisely the vantage point we have been guided to by the speaker.

The spectacle of these "wanton Maidens" splashing in their jasper-bottomed lake surrounded by laurels for protection from the full sun is perhaps too completely narrated to be strictly pictorial. Much of the sensuous visual force derives instead from its appearance at the climax of a cumulative pictorial sequence, and from Spenser's introduction of the motif of enticing half-concealment. This paradox now resonates against other metaphorical opposites displayed in the Bowre: art versus nature, illusion versus reality, covert pleasure versus open enjoyment. A multiplicity of visual detail supports the sensuousness of the narrative in many ways, but more than one example would be luxurious. Here Spenser's figurative veil of waves which both conceal and reveal adumbrates Acrasia's magically veiled appearance a few stanzas later and recalls the "shapes of naked boyes" that seem to move over the fountain:

> Sometimes the one would lift the other quight
> Aboue the waters, and then downe againe
> Her plong, as ouer maistered by might,
> Where both awhile would couered remaine,
> And each the other from to rise restraine;
> The whiles their snowy limbes, as through a vele,
> So through the Christall waues appeared plaine:
> Then suddeinly both would themselues vnhele,
> And th'amarous sweet spoiles to greedy eyes reuele.
>
> (2.12.64)

The whole scene is made to catch "greedy eyes," and the Palmer's conspicuous absence perhaps implies that such eyes alone—obviously, including ours—are in danger.

Much of this stanza and the next two, as well as the whole of sixty-seven, is a direct translation of Tasso's *Gerusalemme liberata.* Yet Tasso, almost as an aside, puts the bathers in a natural or apparently natural pool, not against the wrought and heightened background they have in *The Faerie Queene.* Once Spenser has provided a setting, he might, like Tasso, concentrate upon the alluring tactics of the nymphs, but he inverts the order of stanzas so that Tasso's chief simile (15.60), instead of exactly illustrating one girl's deliberate rise from the water to display herself, elaborates the continuing imagery of "christalline humour" that pervades this section of the Bowre:

> As that faire Starre, the messenger of morne,
> His deawy face out of the sea doth reare:
> Or as the *Cyprian* goddesse, newly borne
> Of the'Oceans fruitfull froth, did first appeare:
> Such seemed they, and so their yellow heare
> Christalline humour dropped downe apace.
>
> (2.12.65)

> Qual matutina stella esce de l'onde
> rugiadosa e stillante, o come fuore
> spuntò nascendo già da le feconde
> spume de l'ocean la dea d'amore,
> tal apparve costei, tal le sue bionde
> chiome stillavan cristallino umore.
>
> (15.60)

An image of appearances is the link between Spenser's version and the nymphs in his fountain, so we remain unconcerned that he applies singulars in the simile to two nymphs. He carefully builds his setting and fixes its visual imagery into a cluster before he allows fresh action. Then he reduces dramatic exchange to the minimum of "espying," and laughter is the only sound. As Guyon watches the laughing girls he is allowed merely to "relent his earnest pace" and "secret pleasaunce to embrace." Tasso's imagery is dispersed throughout his knights' dramatic encounter, which ends, unlike Spenser's, with an enticing song of propaganda for the garden. The reflexive action that does remain in Spenser's imitation is partly neutralized by the trick of near repetition in those phrases characterizing Guyon's responses (2.12.65 and 69). The bathers have scarcely noticed Guyon's grave interest when the Palmer "much rebukt those wandring eyes of his,/ And counseld well, him forward thence did draw" (2.12.69).

Spenser's transition to the moment when Acrasia is revealed to Guyon and the Palmer is most foggy. They are guided to her by sound, not sight; but the speaker interrupts in its midst his description of this consort of natural and artificial sounds to tell the audience that Acrasia, with her lover "In secret shade, after long wanton ioyes," is at the source of the music, "Whilst round about them pleasauntly did sing/ Many faire Ladies, and lasciuious boyes" (2.12.72). Spenser's seemingly purposeful fragmentation of experience neutralizes the sense of drama that Tasso cultivates in canto XVI of *Gerusalemme liberata*. Music surrounds Tasso's searchers as they move through Armida's garden, but his account follows them directly through the enchanted paradise until they see her with Rinaldo; then Tasso describes Armida's appearance and her attendance on Rinaldo. However, in Acrasia's garden action seems discontinuous, even unimportant. Like space, action is shattered, displaced, and subverted: in each of his encounters Guyon meets a figure playing out an eternal role in the Bowre, but only Guyon's action has any temporality—seeing the gates and overthrowing the Genius, seeing the porch hung with grapes and breaking the cup of Excesse, admiring the fountain and its threatening bathers.

Acrasia's action, which is as eternal as Excesse's offer of the cup "to each,/ Whom passing by she happened to meet," is first presented to the reader as an aside, not as part of a sustained narrative of Guyon's moment-to-moment experience.

This vignette is a privileged glance which neutralizes any suspense the reader may feel:

> And all that while, right ouer him she hong,
> With her false eyes fast fixed in his sight,
> As seeking medicine, whence she was stong,
> Or greedily depasturing delight:
> And oft inclining downe with kisses light,
> For feare of waking him, his lips bedewd,
> And through his humid eyes did sucke his spright,
> Quite molten into lust and pleasure lewd;
> Wherewith she sighed soft, as if his case she rewd.
>
> (2.12.73)

Spenser tells us not so much how Acrasia looks as what she does to Verdant; the visual details are reserved for Guyon's and the Palmer's encounter with her. Music immediately continues with the famous song, "So passeth, in the passing of a day," translated from Tasso (2.12.74-75). The vignette of Acrasia and Verdant is suspended in music, and is spatially disjoined from other elements of the Bowre. When Guyon and the Palmer do at last pass through this musical surrogate of space and see Acrasia with Verdant just as the singer finishes, a curtain seems suddenly to have opened on a tableau appearing at the end of a walk down a long, dark, music-filled hall:

> He ceast, and then gan all the quire of birdes
> Their diuerse notes t'attune vnto his lay,
> As in approuance of his pleasing words.
> The constant paire heard all, that he did say,
> Yet swarued not, but kept their forward way,
> Through many couert groues, and thickets close,
> In which they creeping did at last display
> That wanton Ladie, with her louer lose,
> Whose sleepie head she in her lap did soft dispose.
>
> (2.12.76)

Illusion in the Bowre of Blisse

Tasso's treatment of space at a similar juncture in the journey through Armida's garden is just different enough to call attention to odd arrangement of space in the Bowre of Blisse. Armida and Rinaldo are not suddenly revealed to the searching knights, but are first seen indistinctly through the leaves of a forest saturated with music. Tasso strives for a sense of distance and atmospheric perspective entirely absent in Spenser's preparation for the tableau of Acrasia:

> Fra melodia sì tenera, fra tante
> vaghezze allettatrici e lusinghiere,
> va quella coppia, e rigida e costante
> se stessa indura a i vezzi del piacere.
> Ecco tra fronde e fronde il guardo inante
> penetra e vede, o pargli di vedere,
> vede pur certo il vago e la diletta,
> ch'egli è in grembo a la donna, essa a l'erbetta.
>
> (16.17)

(Through music so delicate, through so many alluring and enticing beauties, these two go, both firm and constant, hardening themselves to the charms of pleasure. Behold, through leaf upon leaf their glance penetrates before and they see, or seem to see—see quite certainly—the erring lover and his mistress and that she is on the lawn with him in her lap.)[39]

Tasso's lines represent in time and space an action which Spenser summarizes (2.12.76) as a preface to his tableau. Elsewhere in *The Faerie Queene* Spenser does represent action through formally stylized vision—in the frontal type of Scanning for example—but not with Tasso's emphasis on swift narrative progression. After Armida and Rinaldo are discovered, they are described, they speak and act; in the Bowre

---

[39] The Fairfax translation does not reveal this point adequately. This is the author's attempt.

of Blisse Acrasia's single motion, "oft inclining downe with kisses light," has been interpreted for the reader much before in stanza seventy-three. When Guyon and the Palmer finally see her, Verdant is still asleep and Acrasia is simply produced —a magnificent and seductive object.

> Vpon a bed of Roses she was layd,
> As faint through heat, or dight to pleasant sin,
> And was arayd, or rather disarayd,
> All in a vele of silke and siluer thin,
> That hid no whit her alablaster skin,
> But rather shewd more white, if more might bee:
> More subtile web *Arachne* can not spin,
> Nor the fine nets, which oft we wouen see
> Of scorched deaw, do not in th'aire more lightly flee.
>
> Her snowy brest was bare to readie spoyle
> Of hungry eies, which n'ote therewith be fild,
> And yet through languour of her late sweet toyle,
> Few drops, more cleare then Nectar, forth distild,
> That like pure Orient perles adowne it trild,
> And her faire eyes sweet smyling in delight,
> Moystened their fierie beames, with which she thrild
> Fraile harts, yet quenched not; like starry light
> Which sparckling on the silent waues, does seeme
>   more bright.   (2.12.77-78)

I have already discussed in detail Spenser's brilliant Focused imagery in stanza seventy-seven representing an evanescent visual impression of Acrasia (see Chapter Two). Sensuous imagery recalling the fountain is compressed into this remarkably sensual revelation of the enchantress, and Spenser's figurative mimesis of a perceptual struggle with Acrasia's ambiguous appearance becomes for the reader a correlative of her particularly insidious threat to temperance. The imagery in the second of these stanzas is imitated from Tasso but expanded; in Spenser's new context it is directly associated with the transient glitter of "fine nets, which oft we wouen see/ Of scorched deaw." Gone is the physicality of Tasso's contrast between Armida's face heated with passion and the white appearance of the sweat which covers it: "e 'l suo infiammato viso/ fan biancheggiando i bei sudor più vivo."[40] We perceive Acrasia as a nexus of images in which light is refracted through moisture; as we proceed through the Focused image of her gown to the "drops, more cleare then Nectar" on her bosom and finally to her "hungry eies," Acrasia becomes an impalpable projection in hypnotic shifting light. If the "naked Damzelles" are the severest trial of Guyon's "greedy eyes," Acrasia is surely most dangerous for the reader's.

In only one more stanza Verdant is quickly described, and the Palmer captures both lovers in his "subtile net." In the Bowre of Blisse Acrasia and Verdant, unlike Armida and Rinaldo in Tasso's garden, do not act and speak, but are silently presented as if set up to be caught in the net. Such

---

[40] See *Opere, III*, 530n. This is the stanza from Tasso:

> Ella dinanzi al petto ha il vel diviso,
> e 'l crin sparge incomposto al vento estivo;
> langue per vezzo, e 'l suo infiammato viso
> fan biancheggiando i bei sudor più vivo:
> qual raggio in onda, le scintilla un riso
> ne gli umidi occhi tremulo e lascivo.
> Sovra lui pende; ed ei nel grembo molle
> le posa il capo, e 'l volto al volto attolle. (16.18)

> Her breasts were naked, for the day was hot,
> Her locks unbound wav'd in the wanton wind;
> Some deal she sweat, (tir'd with the game you wot),
> Her sweat-drops bright, white, round, like pearls of Inde;
> Her humid eyes a fiery smile forth shot,
> That like sun-beams in silver fountains shin'd;
> O'er him her looks she hung, and her soft breast
> The pillow was where he and love took rest.

stylized relationships between setting and action exist through-
out the episode. The entire Bowre is arranged to be alluring,
and it is touched liberally with vivid descriptive and pictorial
imagery. Yet its fragmentary and discontinuous spatial or-
ganization holds us at a distance and forces us to a rigorous
examination of surfaces. Spenser seems to be uneasy with
perspective space, and even to distrust it. He apparently does
not want the Bowre's destruction to be too moving, so he
balances fully spatialized settings and pictorial images against
others that are more obviously conventional. Of course his
imagery is controlled throughout by moral judgments that
are integral to his verbal medium. Still, the images are potent,
and, even though Guyon has passed his crisis and the Palmer
is invulnerable, it is remarkable that the destruction is so swift:

> But all those pleasant bowres and Pallace braue,
> *Guyon* broke downe, with rigour pittilesse;
> Ne ought their goodly workmanship might saue
> Them from the tempest of his wrathfulnesse,
> But that their blisse he turn'd to balefulnesse:
> Their groues he feld, their gardins did deface,
> Their arbers spoyle, their Cabinets suppresse,
> Their banket houses burne, their buildings race,
> And of the fairest late, now made the fowlest place.
>
> (2.12.83)

How can statement overpower image? Readers have often
argued that these images cannot be so easily broken in their
imaginations. I feel that Spenser attempted to create those
images out of such a verbal texture and to place them at such
a distance that their destructibility would be assured and
justified. He weighs alluring immediacy of detail against
patent spatial artificiality in order to reveal how wrongly-
motivated art inspires vice: art can make things appear as
they really are, but also as they really are not. He *shows* the

dangers of Acrasia's amoral aesthetic. If Spenser has achieved such a balance—if he has managed to set Faerie Land at a distance, to idealize it, to make it heroic, and also to touch it with immediate pictorial detail—the precarious harmony can be maintained only in the responses of an audience alert to perceptual experience in the poem and responsive to its rhetoric.

Alciati, Andrea. *Emblemata . . . cvm Commentariis . . . per Clavdivm Minoem.* Antwerp, 1577.

——. *Emblematum Flumen Abundans: or, Alciat's Emblems in their Full Stream,* ed. Henry Green. The Holbein Society's Facsimile Reprints, v. Manchester, 1871.

Allen, Don Cameron. "Muiopotmos, or The Fate of the Butterflie," *Image and Meaning: Metaphoric Traditions in Renaissance Poetry.* Baltimore, 1960.

——. "Symbolic Color in the Literature of the English Renaissance," *PQ,* xv (1936), 81-92.

Alpers, Paul J. "Narrative and Rhetoric in the *Faerie Queene,*" *SEL,* ii (1962), 27-46.

——. *The Poetry of The Faerie Queene.* Princeton, 1967.

Aptekar, Jane. *Icons of Justice: Iconography and Thematic Imagery in Book V of The Faerie Queene.* New York and London, 1969.

Ardizzoni, Anthos. ΠΟΙΗΜΑ: *Ricerche sulla teoria del linguaggio poetico nell'antichità.* Bari, 1953.

Ariosto, Ludovico. *Orlando Fvrioso in English Heroical Verse,* trans. John Harington. London, 1591.

Arnheim, Rudolf. *Art and Visual Perception.* Berkeley and Los Angeles, 1954.

Auerbach, Eric. " 'Figura,' " in *Scenes from the Drama of European Literature.* New York, 1959.

——. *Mimesis: The Representation of Reality in Western Literature,* trans. Willard R. Trask. Princeton, 1953.

Baroway, Israel. "The Imagery of Spenser and the *Song of Songs,*" *JEGP,* xxxiii (1934), 23-45.

Benesch, Otto. *The Art of the Renaissance in Northern Europe.* Cambridge, Mass., 1945.

Bennett, Josephine Waters. *The Evolution of "The Faerie Queene."* Chicago, 1942.

Bibliography

Berger, Harry, Jr. *The Allegorical Temper: Vision and Reality in Book II of Spenser's Faerie Queene.* New Haven, 1957.

Binyon, Laurence. "English Poetry in Its Relation to Painting and the Other Arts," *Proceedings of the British Academy,* VIII (1917-1918), 381-402.

Bloomfield, Morton W. "Authenticating Realism and the Realism of Chaucer," *Thought,* XXXIX (1964), 335-358.

——. *The Seven Deadly Sins.* n.p.: Michigan State College Press, 1952.

——. "Symbolism in Medieval Literature," *MP,* LVI (1958), 73-81.

Blunt, Sir Anthony. *Artistic Theory in Italy 1450-1600.* Oxford, 1940 and 1962.

Boas, George. [Review of Art and Illusion], *JAAC,* XIX (1960-1961), 229.

Brink, C. O. *Horace on Poetry.* Cambridge, 1963.

Bruyne, Edgar de. *Études d'Esthétique Médiévale,* 3 vols. Bruges, 1946.

Bundy, Murray Wright. *The Theory of Imagination in Classical and Medieval Thought.* University of Illinois Studies in Language and Literature, XII (1927).

Bush, Douglas. *Mythology and the Renaissance Tradition in English Poetry.* Minneapolis, 1932.

Buswell, Guy T. *How People Look at Pictures.* Chicago, 1935.

Buxton, John. *Elizabethan Taste.* London, 1963.

Castelvetro, Lodovico. *Poetica d'Aristotele vulgarizzata et sposta.* Basel, 1576.

Charlton, H. B. *Castelvetro's Theory of Poetry.* Manchester, 1913.

Chew, Samuel C. *The Pilgrimage of Life.* New Haven, 1962.

Clements, Robert J. *Picta Poesis: Literary and Humanistic Theory in Renaissance Emblem Books.* Rome, 1960.

Colie, Rosalie L. *Paradoxia Epidemica: The Renaissance Tradition of Paradox.* Princeton, 1966.

Dallett, Joseph B. "Ideas of Sight in *The Faerie Queene*," *ELH*, xxvii (1960), 87-121.

Damon, Phillip. "History and Idea in Renaissance Criticism," in *Literary Criticism and Historical Understanding: Selected Papers from the English Institute*, ed. Phillip Damon. New York and London, 1967.

Davis, B.E.C. *Edmund Spenser*. Cambridge, 1933. Reprinted, New York, 1962.

Dolce, Lodovico. *Aretino: a Dialogue on Painting*. Glasgow, 1770.

Durling, Robert M. *The Figure of the Poet in Renaissance Epic*. Cambridge, Mass., 1965.

Elliott, John R., Jr., ed. *The Prince of Poets: Essays on Edmund Spenser*. New York and London, 1968.

Empson, William. *Seven Types of Ambiguity*, 2nd ed. London, 1947.

Fairchild, Arthur H. R. *Shakespeare and the Arts of Design*. University of Missouri Studies, xii. Columbia, Mo., 1937.

Fletcher, Angus. *Allegory: The Theory of a Symbolic Mode*. Ithaca, 1964.

Fletcher, Jefferson B. "The Painter of the Poets," *SP*, xiv (1917), 153-166.

Frank, Joseph. "Spatial Form in Modern Literature," in *The Widening Gyre*. New Brunswick, N.J., 1963.

Freeman, Rosemary. *English Emblem Books*. London, 1948.

Frey, Dagobert. *Gotik und Renaissance als Grundlagen der modernen Weltanschauung*. Augsburg, 1929.

Galilei, Galileo. *Scritti letterari*, ed. Alberto Chiari. Florence, 1943.

Giamatti, A. Bartlett. *The Earthly Paradise and the Renaissance Epic*. Princeton, 1966.

Gibson, James J. *The Perception of the Visual World*. Boston, 1950.

Gibson, James J. "The Visual Field and the Visual World," *Psychological Review*, LIX (1952), 148-151, 246-247.

———. "Pictures, Perspective, and Perception," *Daedalus*, LXXXIX (1960), 216-217.

Giovannini, Giovanni. "Method in the Study of Literature and Its Relation to the Other Arts," *JAAC*, VIII (1950), 185-195.

Giovio, Paolo. *The Worthy Tract of Paulus Iovius Contayning a Discourse of Rare Inventions . . . Called Impresse*, trans. Samuel Daniel. London, 1585.

Glazier, Lyle. "The Nature of Spenser's Imagery," *MLQ*, XVI (1955), 300-310.

Gombrich, E. H. *Art and Illusion*. Princeton, 1959. 2nd ed., 1961.

———. "*Icones Symbolicae*: The Visual Image in Neo-Platonic Thought," *JWCI*, XI (1948), 163-192.

———. "Lessing (Lecture on a Master Mind)," *Proceedings of the British Academy*, XLIII (1957), 133-156.

———. "Moment and Movement in Art," *JWCI*, XXVII (1964), 293-306.

Gottfried, Rudolf. "The Pictorial Element in Spenser's Poetry," *ELH*, XIX (1952), 203-213.

Green, Henry. *Shakespeare and the Emblem Writers*. London, 1870.

Greene, Thomas M. "Spenser and the Epithalamic Convention," *CL*, IX (1957), 215-228.

Hagstrum, Jean H. *The Sister Arts*. Chicago and London, 1958.

Hamilton, A. C. *The Structure of Allegory in The Faerie Queene*. Oxford, 1961.

Hard, Frederick. "Spenser's 'Clothes of Arras and of Toure,'" *SP*, XXVII (1930), 162-185.

Hathaway, Baxter. *The Age of Criticism: The Late Renaissance in Italy*. Ithaca, 1962.

Hind, Arthur M. *Engraving in England in the Sixteenth and Seventeenth Centuries,* I, "The Tudor Period." Cambridge, 1952.

Honig, Edwin. *Dark Conceit.* Evanston, 1959.

Hoskins, John. *Directions for Speech and Style,* ed. Hoyt H. Hudson. Princeton, 1935.

Jack, Ian. *Keats and the Mirror of Art.* Oxford, 1967.

Kaske, R. E. "Chaucer and Medieval Allegory," *ELH,* xxx (1963), 175-192.

Kermode, Frank. "The Cave of Mammon," *Elizabethan Poetry: Stratford-upon-Avon Studies,* II (1960), 150-173. Reprinted in *The Prince of Poets,* pp. 256-286 (see above, Elliott).

Kingsford, Charles L. "Essex House, formerly Leicester House and Exeter Inn," *Archaeologia,* LXXIII (1923), 1-54.

Krieger, Murray. "*Ekphrasis* and the Still Movement of Poetry; or *Laokoön* Revisited," in *Perspectives on Poetry,* ed. James L. Calderwood and Harold E. Toliver, pp. 323-348. New York, 1968.

Kris, Ernst. *Psychoanalytic Explorations in Art.* New York, 1952.

Langdon, Ida. *Materials for a Study of Spenser's Theory of Fine Art.* Ithaca, 1911.

Larrabee, Stephen A. "Fine Arts and Poetry" and "Ut Pictura Poesis," in *Princeton Encyclopedia of Poetry and Poetics,* ed. Alex Preminger, pp. 274-276 and 881-883. Princeton, 1965.

————. *English Bards and Grecian Marbles: The Relationship between Sculpture and Poetry Especially in the Romantic Period.* New York, 1943.

Lee, Rensselaer W. "*Ut Pictura Poesis*: The Humanistic Theory of Painting," *Art Bulletin,* XXII (1940), 197-269. Reprinted as a book, New York, 1967.

Bibliography

Leonardo da Vinci. *Leonardo: omo sanza lettere*, ed. Giuseppina Fumagalli. Florence, 1952.

Lessing, G. E. *Laocoön*, trans. Edward A. McCormick. New York, 1962.

————. *Laokoön*, ed. Dorothy Reich. Oxford, 1965.

Levey, Michael. *The Later Italian Pictures in the Collection of Her Majesty the Queen.* London, 1964.

Lewis, C. S. *The Allegory of Love.* New York, 1958.

Lomazzo, G. P. *Trattato dell'arte della pittura, scultura, et architettura.* Milan, 1584.

————. *Tracte Containing the Artes of Curious Paintinge, Carvinge & Buildinge . . .* , trans. R. H. [Richard Haydocke]. Oxford, 1598.

Lotspeich, Henry Gibbons. *Classical Mythology in the Poetry of Edmund Spenser.* Princeton, 1932. Reprinted, New York, 1965.

Mâle, Emile. *The Gothic Image*, trans. Dora Nussey. New York, 1958.

Mazzeo, Joseph A. "A Critique of Some Modern Theories of Metaphysical Poetry," in *Seventeenth Century English Poetry*, ed. William R. Keast. New York, 1962.

Mercer, Eric. "The Decoration of the Royal Palaces from 1553-1625," *Archaeological Journal*, cx (1953), 150-163.

————. *English Art, 1553-1625.* Oxford, 1962.

Millar, Oliver. *The Tudor, Stuart, and Early Georgian Pictures in the Collection of Her Majesty the Queen.* 2 vols. London, 1963.

Ong, Walter J. "From Allegory to Diagram in the Renaissance Mind: a Study in the Significance of the Allegorical Tableau," *JAAC*, xvii (1958-1959), 423-440.

————. "System, Space, and Intellect in Renaissance Symbolism," *Bibliothèque d'Humanisme et Renaissance*, xviii (1956), 222-239.

Owen, W.J.B. "The Structure of *The Faerie Queene*," *PMLA*, LXVIII (1953), 1079-1100.

Panofsky, Erwin. *Galileo as a Critic of the Arts*. The Hague, 1954.

——. *Idea: Ein Beitrag zur Begriffsgeschichte der älteren Kunsttheorie*. Leipzig, 1924. 2nd ed., Berlin, 1960. Trans. Joseph J. S. Peake, Columbia, S.C., 1968.

——. *The Life and Art of Albrecht Dürer*. Princeton, 1955.

——. *Meaning in the Visual Arts*. Garden City, N.Y., 1955.

——. *Renaissance and Renascences in Western Art*, 2 vols. Copenhagen, 1960.

——. *Studies in Iconology*. New York, 1939 and 1962.

Park, Roy. "'*Ut Pictura Poesis*': The Nineteenth-Century Aftermath," *JAAC*, XXVIII (1969), 155-164.

Peacham, Henry. *The Garden of Eloqvence*. London, 1577.

——. *The Garden of Eloqvence* .... *Corrected and Augmented by the first Author*. London, 1593.

Pope-Hennessy, John. "Nicholas Hilliard and Mannerist Art Theory," *JWCI*, VI (1943), 89-100.

Praz, Mario. *The Flaming Heart*. Garden City, N.Y., 1958.

——. "[Emblems and Insignia] Medieval Through Modern West," *Encyclopedia of World Art*, IV. New York, 1961.

——. "Milton e Poussin," *Gusto Neoclassico*, 2nd ed. Naples, 1959. Also in *Seventeenth Century Studies Presented to Sir Herbert Grierson*. Oxford, 1938.

——. *Mnemosyne: the Parallel between Literature and the Visual Arts*. Princeton, 1970.

——. *Studies in Seventeenth Century Imagery*. 2 vols. London, 1939. 2nd ed., enlarged. Rome, 1964.

Puttenham, George. *The Arte of English Poesie*, ed. Gladys Doidge Willcock and Alice Walker. Cambridge, 1936.

Robertson, D. W., Jr. *A Preface to Chaucer*. Princeton, 1962.

Roche, Thomas P., Jr. *The Kindly Flame: A Study of the*

Third and Fourth Books of Spenser's Faerie Queene. Princeton, 1964.

Rudenstine, Neil L. *Sidney's Poetic Development.* Cambridge, Mass., 1967.

Sale, Roger. *Reading Spenser: An Introduction to The Faerie Queene.* New York, 1968.

Satterthwaite, Alfred W. *Spenser, Ronsard, and DuBellay.* Princeton, 1960.

Scharr, Claes. *The Golden Mirror: Studies in Chaucer's Descriptive Technique and Its Literary Background.* Lund, 1955.

Smith, Barbara Herrnstein. *Poetic Closure.* Chicago and London, 1968.

Smith, Hallett. "The Use of Conventions in Spenser's Minor Poems," pp. 122-145 in *Form and Convention in the Poetry of Edmund Spenser,* ed. William Nelson. New York and London, 1961.

Sonn, Carl Robinson. "Spenser's Imagery," *ELH,* xxvi (1959), 156-170.

Souriau, Étienne. "Time in the Plastic Arts," *JAAC,* vii (1949), 294-307.

Spencer, John R. "*Ut Rhetorica Pictura,* A Study in Quattrocento Theory of Painting," *JWCI,* xx (1957), 26-44.

Spenser, Edmund. *Complaints,* ed. W. L. Renwick. London, 1928.

———. *Daphnaïda and Other Poems,* ed. W. L. Renwick. London, 1929.

———. *The Works of Spenser: A Variorum Edition,* ed. Edwin Greenlaw, Charles G. Osgood, Frederick M. Padelford, *et al.* 11 vols. Baltimore, 1932-1957.

Stallman, Robert. "Keats the Apollonian: the Time-and-Space Logic of His Poems as Paintings," *UTQ,* xvi (1947), 143-156.

Steadman, John M. "Spenser's House of Care: a Reinterpretation," *SRen*, VII (1960), 207-224.

Stein, Harold. *Studies in Spenser's Complaints*. New York, 1934.

Strong, Roy C. *The English Icon: Elizabethan and Jacobean Portraiture*. London and New York, 1969.

———. *Portraits of Queen Elizabeth I*. Oxford, 1963.

———. *Tudor and Jacobean Portraits*, 2 vols. London, 1969.

Sugden, Herbert W. *The Grammar of Spenser's Faerie Queene*. Language Dissertations Published by the Linguistic Society of America, No. 22. Philadelphia, 1936.

Sutton, Walter. "The Literary Image and the Reader: a Consideration of the Theory of Spatial Form," *JAAC*, XVI (1957-58), 112-123.

Sypher, Wylie. *Four Stages of Renaissance Style*. Garden City, N.Y., 1955.

That Soueraine Light, Essays in Honor of Edmund Spenser, 1552-1952, ed. William R. Mueller and Don Cameron Allen. Baltimore, 1952.

Thoms, William J. "Pictures of the Great Earl of Leicester," *NQ*, 3rd ser., II (1862), 201-202 and 224-226.

Tuve, Rosemond. *Allegorical Imagery: Some Medieval Books and Their Posterity*. Princeton, 1966.

———. "Baroque and Mannerist Milton?" *Milton Studies in Honor of H. F. Fletcher*. Urbana, 1961.

———. *Elizabethan and Metaphysical Imagery*. Chicago, 1947.

———. *Essays by Rosemond Tuve*, ed. Thomas P. Roche, Jr. Princeton, 1970.

———. "Spenser and Mediaeval Mazers; with a Note on Jason in Ivory," *SP*, XXXIV (1937), 138-147.

———. "Spenser and Some Pictorial Conventions," *SP*, XXXVII (1940), 149-176.

Vernon, M. D. *The Psychology of Perception*. Baltimore, 1962.

Volkmann, Ludwig. *Bilderschriften der Renaissance: Hieroglyphik und Emblematik in Ihren Beziehungen und Fortwirkungen.* Leipzig, 1923.

Wahl, Marcelle. *Création Picturale et Ordre Cérébral.* Paris, 1964.

Waterhouse, Ellis. *Painting in Britain 1530-1790.* London, 1953.

———. "Tasso and the Visual Arts," *Italian Studies,* III (1947-48), 146-162.

Watkins, W.B.C. *Shakespeare and Spenser.* Princeton, 1950.

Weinberg, Bernard. "Castelvetro's Theory of Poetics," in *Critics and Criticism,* ed. R. S. Crane. Chicago, 1952.

———. *A History of Literary Criticism in the Italian Renaissance.* 2 vols. Chicago, 1961.

———. "Poetry and Poetic Theory in the Italian Renaissance," *UTQ,* XXXI (1962), 283-298.

Weitzmann, Kurt. "Narration in Early Christendom," *American Journal of Archaeology,* LXI (1957), 83-91.

Wellek, René. *A History of Modern Criticism: 1750-1950,* I, "The Later Eighteenth Century." New Haven, 1955.

———. "The Parallelism Between Literature and the Arts," *English Institute Annual,* 1941. New York, 1942.

White, John. *The Birth and Rebirth of Pictorial Space.* London, 1957.

Whitney, Geoffrey. *A Choice of Emblemes, and Other Devices . . . .* Leyden, 1586. Ed. Henry Green as *Whitney's "Choice of Emblems."* London, 1866.

Williams, Kathleen. *Spenser's World of Glass.* Berkeley and Los Angeles, 1966.

Wimsatt, W. K., Jr. *The Verbal Icon: Studies in the Meaning of Poetry.* New York, 1962.

Wölfflin, Heinrich. *Principles of Art History,* trans. M. D. Hottinger. New York: Dover Publications, n.d.

Worringer, Wilhelm. *Form in Gothic,* ed. Herbert Read. London, 1927.

Yates, Frances A. *Allegorical Portraits of Queen Elizabeth I at Hatfield House.* Hatfield, 1952.

———. *The Art of Memory.* Chicago and London, 1966.

———. "Boissard's Costume Book and Two Portraits," *JWCI,* xxii (1959), 365-366.

———. "Elizabethan Chivalry: The Romance of the Accession Day Tilts," *JWCI,* xx (1957), 4-25.

———. "The Emblematic Conceit in Giordano Bruno's *De Gli Eroici Furori* and in the Elizabethan Sonnet Sequences," *JWCI,* vi (1943), 101-121.

———. "Queen Elizabeth as Astraea," *JWCI,* x (1947), 27-82.

INDEX

In this index 44f means separate references on pp. 44 and 45; 44ff means separate references on pp. 44, 45, and 46; 44-46 means a continuous discussion. *Passim*, meaning "here and there," is used for a cluster of references in close but not consecutive sequence.

Index

Index

Index

Legend of Good Women, The, 50-51

Leicester, Earl of, 21n, 155, 174

Leonardo da Vinci, 13n

Lessing, G. E., 3, 13-16, 20, 22, 31

"Letter to Raleigh," 47, 111

Lorrain, Claude, 31

Lotspeich, Henry Gibbons, 179n

Lucifer, 131

Lucifera, 109, 158; approaching, 105ff, 109, 113, 120, 123-34, 139

Madame Bovary, 92-95

Malbecco's castle, 56, 59, 61

Maluenù, 125, 127

Mammon, 136, 138, 142f; Cave of, 105, 134-48, 158

Mannerist art, 19, 147n-48n

manuscripts, illuminated, 21n, 155

Marfisa, 53-54, 56

Marlowe, Christopher, 116n

Mars, 43

"martello d'amore," 103f

Medea, 177, 179f

medieval, see Middle Ages, the

memory: Gombrich on, 25-26; and Keats, 30; art of, 143-44

Merchant of Venice, The, 87-88

Mercilla, 161

metaphor, 40, 53, 85f; Ariosto's, 39, 55; Spenser's, 45, 48, 61, 65, 164, 171-72, 180, 189

Metaphor (rhetorical figure), 84

Michelangelo, 131, 155

Middle Ages, the: books and manuscripts of, 21n, 108-10, 155; and Spenser, 48, 53, 74, 108-12, 142, 147-48; art of, 52-53, 110-11, 120n, 144-45; revival of, 66, 147-48; forms in Scanning, 108-12

Milton, John, 19n, 130; Paradise Lost, 58-60; Paradise Regained, 34

Mimesis, 108

Minerva, 57, 58n, 165-67

"Moment and Movement in Art," 24, 25, 27

Monet, Claude, 129

Motto (Lemma or Vox), 81n

motto: and emblem, 81n, 82, 86-87, 99n, 151, 155. See also "Word"

Mount Acidale, 121, 135, 146, 180

Muiopotmos, 154, 168; butterfly, image of, 162-67, 172

Mulla, Nymphs of, 169

music: and poetry, 16n, 26, 100

mythology, Spenser's use of, 65, 112; in The Faerie Queene, 43, 57, 58n; 122f, 129-32, 141, 179, 182f; in The Shepheardes Calender, 159; in Muiopotmos, 163-68; in Prothalamion, 175

narrative structure and style, 33, 176; and Focusing, 41, 44, 54f; Ariosto's, 54f, 119n; and Framing, 69; continuous narrative method, 106, 110-11, 120, 145n, 166, 185; and Scanning, 108, 110; Spenser's, 119-20, 176, 189; Tasso's, 119-20

Nature, 10, 31f

Negative Capability, 30, 31n

Neo-Medievalism, 66, 147-48

Neoplatonic philosophy, 112

Neptune, 165f

optical illusion, 22

oratory, 8

Orlando furioso, 11, 43-44, 53-56, 67, 97; Alcina, 35-40, 44-45, 53, 56, 115; Marfisa, 53-54, 56; Bradamante, 54-56. See also Ariosto, Ludovico

Orlando innamorato, 57

Ovid, 49, 164-65, 167

215

Index

painting: relationship between poetry and, 3-31, 106f, 112, 128-29, 135, 145n; illusionistic, 27f, 180; passage of time in, 23, 25-26, 100; and Ariosto, 35-36, 38, 40; framing of, 68; continuous narrative method in, 106, 110-11, 120, 145n, 185; primitive, 144; illusion of simultaneity in, 146

Palmer, the, 41, 132, 177, 182, 188-96 *passim*

Panofsky, Erwin, 81n-82n, 83n-84n

Paradise Lost, 58-60

Paradise Regained, 34

"Parallel of Poetry and Painting," 5, 16

Paridell, 58

Parliament of Fowls, The, 49

Peacham, Henry, 38, 151

perspective, 144-45, 146n; and Shakespeare, 97; and Spenser, 128, 145-46, 196

Petrarch, 72, 149, 150n; and emblematic conceits, 64, 82ff

Phaeton, 107, 129-34 *passim*

Philostratus, 8n

Phoebus, 107, 112, 126, 158f

photography, 100, 108, 113; television, 25f; cinema, 26, 106, 108, 114

pictorialism, 3f, 16, 23-31, 175-97; and description, 32-67; in the earlier poems, 149-62; in the minor poems, 162-75. *See also* Focusing; Framing; Scanning

Piers Plowman, 99n

Pilate, 142

Plato, 15n, 67

Plutarch, 8n

poem, long, *see* epic

poema (short poem), 8n

poetry: relationship to painting, 3-31, 106f, 112, 128-29, 135,

145n; illusionistic, 15; and continuous narrative method, 106, 110-11, 120, 145n, 166, 185; argumentative, 158. *See also* description; pictorialism

Pope, Alexander, 16, 17n; *Windsor Forest*, 32

Portia, 87-88

post-medievalism: and Spenser, 53, 110f, 145, 148. *See also* Renaissance, the

Praz, Mario, 5n, 150n, 152n

Prospero, 96

Prothalamion, 149, 162, 172-75; swans, image of, 90-92, 172, 174

Prudence, 143n

punctum temporis, 25f

puns: Spenser's use of, 64, 102f, 161, 169

Puttenham, George, 38, 51, 170

Quintilian, 10n

Raphael, 147n

Redcrosse, 109, 127f, 134

Rembrandt, 13n

Renaissance, the, 108-12, 142-47 *passim*; commonplaces, 3-22, 151n; art of, 52-53, 98, 144-45; and Spenser, 20-22, 48, 53, 72, 74, 110f, 142, 147f, 166n, 169, 172; and emblems, 80, 82n, 83-84, 151, 153n

Renwick, W. L., 17n, 166

Reynolds, John, 30

Rinaldo, 11, 191, 193, 195

Robertson, D. W., Jr., 46-47, 49, 52n

Roche, Thomas P., Jr., 35, 72

Romance, the, 111-12, 176

Rubens, Peter Paul, 16f

Ruggiero, 44-45, 57

Ruines of Time, The, 154, 156-57

Index

Index